Skyscrapers
The New Millennium

Skyscrapers

The New Millennium

Edited by
John Zukowsky
and
Martha Thorne

Prestel

Munich · London · New York

The Art Institute of Chicago

4

Contents

Europe

Middle East

Acknowledgments

A book of this type would have been impossible without the assistance of a great number of people. First and foremost, we thank Tamsen Anderson and Anna Minta for their tireless work in compiling information and writing the draft entries for our survey. Tamsen Anderson also authored the architects' biographies at the end of the book, with some compilation assistance from Jack Neuner. Kathryn Burgomaster completed the work begun by them. All of us were assisted in our efforts by a variety of people from the offices of architects and developers whose work is represented in this book.

We are especially grateful to the following staff members of those firms who were particularly cooperative in supplying photographs and other documentation on their buildings: Eiko Behrens and Petra Eggebrecht of Architekten Kollhoff & Timmermann; Dennis Wilhelm of Arquitectonica; Etienne Piérrès of Atelier Christian de Portzamparc; William D. Chilton of Ellerbe Becket; Wendy Binioris and Stefanie Miller of Brennan Beer Gorman/ Architects; Sarah Gibson of The John Buck Company; Brian Billingsley and Christine Strauss of Busby + Associates Architects; Renate Schweiger of Callison Architecture; Petra Trefalt of Coop Himmelb(l)au; Nazan Yuksel and Terry Mason of Denton Corker Marshall; Avi Lothan of DeStefano & Partners; Scott Toberman of European American Reality,

Ltd.; Elizabeth Walker, Katy Harris, and Lois McDowell of Foster and Partners; Kirsten Sibilia of Fox & Fowle Architects, P. C.; Caroline Hancock of Michael Graves & Associates; Dr. Kenneth Yeang of T. R. Hamzah & Yeang Sdn Bhd; Angela Hijjas of Hijjas Kasturi Associates; Jan Esche of Ingenhoven Overdiek und Partner; Maggie Wong of Kaplan McLaughlin Diaz; Perry Ketchum of Ketchum Metz, Inc.; Ilona Ryder and Baxter Knowlton of Kohn Pedersen Fox Associates, P. C.; Inga Olze of Köllmann AG; Akiko Sato of Kisho Kurokawa Architects & Associates; Tracy Troutman and Cece McAgy of Lucien Lagrange and Associates; Liby Kwok of Dennis Lau & Ng Chun Man Architects and Engineers (H. K.) Ltd; Connie Garrison of Loebl Schlossmann & Hackl; Edwin Denson and Mike Patten of Lohan Associates; Keith Palmer of Murphy/ Jahn, Inc. Architects; Mamoru Maeda and Naeko Yamamoto of Nikken Sekkei Ltd.; Kathy Sekuledes of NORR, Limited; Petra Geis of Novotny Mähner + Assoziierte; Andreas Rust and Mira de la Fontaine of OFB – Bauvermittlungs- und Gewerbebau-GmbH; Ong Tze Boon of Ong & Ong Architects Pte Ltd; Cecilia Ott of Carlos Ott International; Janet Adams Strong, Dee Christy Briggs, and Laura Boutwell of Pei Cobb Freed & Partners Architects LLP; Mig Halpine and Justin Shigemi of Cesar Pelli & Associates; William Dorge of Perkins & Will; Stefania Canta and Giovanna Gusto of Renzo Piano Building Workshop; Sinn Phoghanyudh

of Plan Architect Co. Ltd.; Dan Shapiro of
Prime/Beitler Development Company, L.L.C.;
Lars Klatte of Rhode Kellermann Wawrowsky;
Toshiya Maeda of Shin Takamatsu Architects
& Associates; Katie Sipthorp of The Richard
Rogers Partnership; Sangeeta Narwani of
RMJM Hong Kong Ltd.; Elizabeth Quebe and
Laurel Goncher-Ward of RTKL Associates Inc.;
Deanna Derrig, Pam Kane, Carilyn Platt, and
Bob Pigatti of Skidmore, Owings & Merrill LLP;
K. Jeffries Sydness of Sydness Architects, P. C.;
Annie Viguier of Jean-Paul Viguier; Claudina
Sula and Violeta Ivanescu of The Webb Zerafa
Menkes Housden Partnership; Charlotte Nord

of Windgard Arkitektkontor, A.B.; Jim Tong
of Wong Tung & Partners; and Sandra Tesolin
of Zeidler Roberts Partnership.

This book is the product of the Ernest R.
Graham Study Center for Architectural
Drawings at The Art Institute of Chicago.
A grant from Julien J. Studley, Inc., with additional funding for the Chicago presentation
from The Graham Foundation for Advanced
Studies in the Fine Arts, supported the creation
of an exhibition—at The Art Institute of Chicago from August 19, 2000 through January
15, 2001—based on the results in this book.

John Zukowsky
Martha Thorne

Skyscrapers Before the New Millennium:
A Question of Boom or Bust

JOHN ZUKOWSKY

Skyscraper! The very word prompts a range of emotional responses, from fascination to fear. People have been intrigued by this architectural form since its inception in the late nineteenth and early twentieth centuries. Today enthusiasts often follow the continuing saga of international efforts to build the world's tallest building. Numerous websites on the Internet are devoted to this topic. Societies such as the Council on Tall Buildings and Urban Habitat settle international disputes as to which is the world's tallest building—rivalries and resultant disagreements that are sure to continue through this millennium (see Epilogue). Despite these supporters—whose enthusiasm often borders on boosterism that otherwise might be associated with sports fans—we suspect there are an equal number of people who would be horrified at the thought of having one of these behemoths built in their neighborhood, thereby catalyzing infrastructure problems such as parking, transportation, and diminished access to local services. In a way, these concerns are no different than those of residents who object to the nearby construction of other large complexes, from prisons to hospitals, universities to airports. An attitude of "not in my backyard" seems to prevail. But, unlike health care, educational, and transportation facilities, skyscrapers are still viewed with a certain amount of awe and civic pride by much of the general public. They evoke a positive image even

though they can have both a positive and negative impact on their urban environment. In this book we survey some of the newest skyscrapers that vie for the title of being the world's tallest building. Besides these, we also discuss buildings that are somewhat smaller, though still high-rise constructions. In all, we present the reader with more than fifty of the latest and most interesting tall buildings that are currently under construction—or recently completed—in an effort to demonstrate the continued importance of this building type in the new millennium. This is truly a global survey, with entries beyond the more predictable and often published projects in Asia, North America, and Europe. For instance, our work incorporates sites as far afield as Saudi Arabia, Lebanon, and the United Arab Emirates as well as Uruguay and Mexico. Additionally, our Epilogue examines the race for the world's tallest building in the first years of the twenty-first century. Before we present this worldwide survey, it might be helpful if we examine some skyscrapers from the 1980s and early 1990s in relation to the socio-economic background that spawned their development.

The speculative economic boom of the 1980s helped to catalyze the construction of a number of high rises throughout cities across the globe, from Tokyo to Los Angeles and Hong Kong to Chicago. European examples include buildings designed in the mid- to late eighties—though not completed until the early to mid-nineties—such as the modernist Barcelona hotel designed by the Chicago office of Skidmore, Owings & Merrill, which opened for the 1992 Olympics there, and the controversial, minimal, glass-towered French National Library in Paris by Dominique Perrault, which did not open until 1996. Some earlier major Asian examples include Norman Foster's striking, 1986 structuralist Bank of Hong Kong, I. M. Pei's sleek 1989 Bank of China, Hong Kong, and Kenzo Tange's 1986–91 City Hall, with its Notre Dame-like towers, in Tokyo. In the United States, the historic birthplace of the skyscraper, these new buildings often took the form of massive classicist or historicist structures approximately forty to sixty stories high. Some, such as Michael Graves's Humana Headquarters in Louisville, Kentucky from 1982, project bold new forms onto the American cityscape (Fig. 1), even though the designer, in this and other instances, asserted that he was attempting to recapture the spirit of the American high rise of the 1920s that had been disrupted by International Style modernism after World War II. Other skyscrapers, such as the speculative office building at 190 South LaSalle Street in Chicago from 1987 (Fig. 2) by John Burgee and Philip Johnson, make direct reference to landmark Chicago School buildings by John Wellborn Root. This is particularly evident in vintage photos of Burnham and Root's Masonic Temple of 1892 (demolished), whose exterior massing clearly prefigures that of the similarly styled 190 South LaSalle. Within the latter (Fig. 3), however, one will find a more eclectic combination of almost dictatorial scale and Renaissance details, to create what Philip Johnson called "…the most lengthy, high, and dignified lobby in the city." These and other contextual buildings done in the spirit of international

1
Michael Graves,
Humana Headquarters,
Louisville, Kentucky, USA,
1982

Postmodernism in the 1980s dotted the globe in a seemingly arbitrary way akin to the potpourri of fantasy skyscrapers presented by the Museum of Contemporary Art in Chicago, and published by Rizzoli, in its popular 1980 exhibition *Late Entries to the Chicago Tribune Tower Competition* (Fig. 4). Contextualism, in

2
John Burgee
and Philip Johnson,
190 South LaSalle Street,
Chicago, Illinois, USA, 1987

particular, became a hallmark of skyscrapers designed in the nineties for many Asian locales. Nevertheless, the exuberant, exorbitant eighties catalyzed the creation of many elaborately detailed large constructions in cities throughout the world. And then came "Black Monday," the stock market crash of November 19, 1987.

As with the Great Depression of the 1930s that followed the more traumatic stock market crash of October 29, 1929, the recession of the early 1990s halted construction of a variety of skyscraper projects in the United States, including Cesar Pelli's 1990 design for the world's tallest building. Miglin-Beitler Tower, proposed for Chicago, was to have been 1,999 feet (609 meters) high (Fig. 5). American architects turned their practices towards expanding markets in Asia and the former Soviet-bloc countries in Eastern Europe (following the fall of the Berlin Wall on November 9, 1989). With economies booming in these countries, and growth rates sometimes projected into the double digits, it was relatively easy for American firms with experience in high-rise construction to find work abroad—as office

vacancy rates soared in cities such as Chicago, Los Angeles, and New York. There were even proposals to build the world's tallest building throughout Asian cities and even in Moscow! On a practical note, many Americans were already building skyscrapers in Europe and Asia in the eighties, so connections to clients there were often already established. We have previously mentioned I. M. Pei and Skidmore, Owings & Merrill, but we could equally cite structures such as Helmut Jahn's Messe Tower in Frankfurt from 1984–91 (Fig. 6)—the tallest building in Europe at 843 feet (257 meters) high—as well as Kohn Pedersen Fox's DG Bank, also in Frankfurt, from 1993, a less-than-close second place at 676 feet (206 meters) high. Incidentally, both were superseded within three years by Foster's Commerzbank (see pp. 110-111) of more than 850 feet (259 meters) in height. His and other buildings within this book are essentially products of these periods of recession and post-recession during the early to mid-1990s, when architects sought and received substantial commissions in countries with developing economies, often in Southeast Asia. All was going well with these projects, and journalists reported on the dramatic changes taking place in those skylines during the mid- to late 1990s. This ranged from the remaking of Shanghai's Pudong Section into an instant city of commercial high rises, to the 1996–97 completion of the world's tallest building—the Petronas Towers in Kuala Lumpur—at 1,483 feet (452 meters) high (see pp. 82-83). Then, in mid- to late 1998, volatile highs and lows in stock markets around the world and dramatic downturns in Asian economies led to the cancellation and indefinite postponement of numerous new office towers throughout Southeast Asia (Fig. 7).

5
Cesar Pelli, proposed Miglin-Beitler Tower (unexecuted),
Chicago, Illinois, USA, 1990

6
Murphy/Jahn Architects,
Messe Tower,
Frankfurt, Germany, 1991

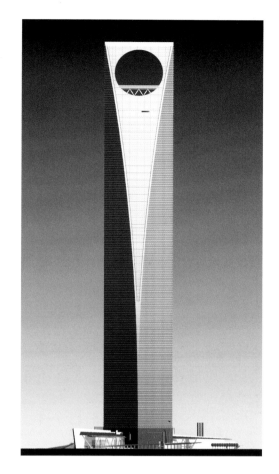

7
Kohn Pedersen Fox,
Shanghai World
Financial Center,
planned completion 2004

The Asian economic tiger was no more, and completed buildings from Shanghai to Kuala Lumpur to Bangkok continue to have only a few tenants. Still, we must realize that all of this runs in cycles. Even if it takes several years for various economies around the world to recuperate, Asian urban landscapes are among those most likely to change dramatically in the new millennium. Despite the Asian downturn, the American cityscape has seen a dynamic resurgence of building since 1997–98, including the construction of midrises ranging from fifteen to twenty stories and the development of plans for full-fledged skyscrapers, including some for the record books (see Epilogue, pp. 122-129). Unlike the international impact of the Great Depression of the 1930s, then, the recessions of the nineties have affected construction in a more regional and sporadic way. Another important development witnessed in the 1990s relates to the technology of skyscrapers, and it might be a good idea to

present at least a few examples here. As in other sectors of contemporary society, the building industry is becoming more concerned with value-oriented or value-engineered products and products that are environmentally friendly. Indeed, there have been several new buildings that address society's interest in the latter (see pp. 36-37, 78-79, 98-100), perhaps the most famous being Foster's 1996 Commerzbank in Frankfurt (see pp. 110-111). But even before that and other constructions of the 1990s, some buildings in the eighties were designed with environmental issues in mind. One prominent example is Nikken Sekkei's 1986–90 NEC Tower in Tokyo (Fig. 8). The headquarters of this electronic corporation, the building was designed to refer to traditional Japanese castle forms, but obviously on a much larger scale. Although its contextualism relates to worldwide design ideas of the time, the building is also a forerunner of the

8
Nikken Sekkei,
NEC Tower,
Tokyo, Japan, 1990

9
Otis "Odyssey"
schematic
diagram

10
SMART System

nineties "green" skyscraper in that it stresses systematic energy conservation with features such as operable airflow windows and heat recovery systems, nighttime heat purging systems, low-energy air and water circulation systems, an extremely efficient zoned air-conditioning, and advanced building main-tenance systems. In short, this is an intelligent building appropriate to the image of a high-tech computer and telecommunications equip-ment company such as NEC. Because of its extensive energy saving features it received several awards in Japan such as the Energy Conservation Architecture Award (1991) and an award from The Society of Heating, Air Conditioning, and Sanitary Engineers of Japan (1992).

Beyond environmental factors, other issues in high-rise construction today relate to practical matters such as the traffic patterns of the occupants and the construction of the building itself. As regards moving people through sky-scrapers, major elevator companies such as

Kone, Otis, and Mitsubishi are developing new systems to increase efficiency in that area. For instance, Kone has developed a "Best Deck" computerized system that enables elevators to be programmed to service floors more frequently during peak traffic times. Otis is developing a new integrated transit system called "Odyssey" featuring an elevator cab that moves both vertically and horizontally, enabling the occupation of an elevator shaft by more than one cab at a time (Fig 9). Although this complex people-mover system is far from being implemented, elevator com-panies are actively investigating the feasibility of triple-deck cabs, moving beyond the double-deck models that exist in certain very tall buildings today. Construction companies such as Shimizu in Japan are also experimenting with the robotic assembly of skyscrapers. Their SMART system, an acronym for "Shimizu Manufacturing System by Advanced Robotics Technology," has been used to build several high rises, up to thirty stories high, in both Yokohama and Nagoya from 1991–97. Within

11
Step Over Tower

their construction system, welding, riveting, and beam placement are all done by computer operators rather than actual laborers, thereby increasing efficiency and reducing construction costs in Japan where labor is expensive (Fig. 10). Other solutions related to earthquake damping and sophisticated wind tunnel modeling are being developed by construction companies in Japan which often have research institutes as part of their businesses. For example, Norman Foster, along with the Obayashi Corporation, planned the 2,600 foot-(792 meter-)high Millennium Tower in 1990 as an answer to the world's tallest building. However, they still use this tower as a design laboratory to develop new structural and spatial forms for their skyscraper designs (see Epilogue, pp. 122-129). The Shimizu company has also developed a theoretical building called the Step Over Tower, a super tower approximately 2,600 feet (792 meters) in height that

12
Christian de Portzamparc, Crédit Lyonnais Tower, Lille, France, 1991–95

13
NORR Limited, and Carlos Ott International, National Bank of Dubai, United Arab Emirates, 1991–98

spans and, thus, preserves the existing urban infrastructure (Fig. 11). Shimizu's research division is also investigating multi-story subterranean constructions, an earthquake-proof "Super High Rise" some 1,787 feet (545 meters) in height, and a "Mega-Truss Pyramidal City" for a million people that is 6,513 feet (1,985 meters) high and recalls theoretical proposals by members of the Japanese Metabolist movement of the 1960s and 1970s.

In all, these latest research efforts of architects, engineers, contractors, and building suppliers demonstrate that ideas concerning the tall office building are alive and percolating within our society, ready to blossom through the new millennium, pending funding by developers and their investors. Our survey that follows is intended to give the reader an idea of the broad selection of skyscrapers that are now being built all over the world, in anticipation of still others that will be constructed

later in the century. The entries for this survey were prepared by Tamsen Anderson and Anna Minta during 1997–98, with the editorial advice of myself and Martha Thorne. We have attempted to provide the reader with a survey as extensive as could possibly fit within these pages, though there are many other projects and buildings that would merit inclusion had we more space and time. These range from significant high rises and individualistic buildings completed in the 1990s (Figs. 12, 13, 14) to striking projects that may or may not proceed, according to funding (Fig. 15). We have grouped the buildings in our book according to geographic clusters so that one can examine them within a local or regional context. We hope that these groupings will offer a rich visual tour of architectural landmarks that will soon exist within various international urban environments in the near future—landmarks that will leave their mark on the ongoing history of this building type, the skyscraper.

14
The Stubbins Associates, Ltd., Landmark Tower, Yokohama, Japan, 1990–93

15
Shin Takematsu, in association with Eliakim Architects, proposed ELA Tower, Tel Aviv, Israel, designed 1995–96

Projects

Two views
of the model

Sheraton Tower at Wall Centre

Architect	Busby + Associates Architects, Vancouver, Canada
Structural Engineer	Glotman Simpson
Client	Wall Financial Corporation
Location	Vancouver, Canada
Date	Estimated construction 1998 – June 2001

Study for the Wall Centre
Garden Hotel, Vancouver

The forty-five-story hotel completes the Wall Centre development that comprises a thirty-four-story hotel and a twenty-nine-story tower for residential use, built during phase I in 1992–93. The curvilinear low-rise podium contains commercial and retail space, and a central landscaped plaza, known as Volunteer Square, connects the new slender hotel tower to the existing buildings.

The hotel is located at the south edge of the downtown business district, with its accumulation of high rises, and, according to his announcement in *The Province*, the developer wanted his hotel tower to become the city's "signature building" (August 27, 1998). The plans for the 450-foot (137-meter) tower immediately provoked a controversial debate on height restriction for downtown buildings. In 1974, to preserve views of the North Shore mountains, the maximum height of a skyscraper had been set at 300 feet (92 meters) with an additional 150 feet (45 meters) at the discretion of the municipality. Although Vancouver has other buildings that are some 450 feet (137 meters) tall, the Sheraton Tower will be the city's tallest building because it stands on the highest point of the downtown peninsula.

The translucent, elliptical tower rises above a 56-foot (17-meter) high lobby that is anchored by a triangular concrete brace around its perimeter, eliminating the need for a conventional central service core. In the atrium, the elevators are constructed of transparent glass that becomes opaque when triggered by an electric impulse at the fifth floor.

The exterior of the Hotel is clad in pale gold, reflective, sintered glass and marked by several double-height garden floors. The external glazing is the outermost component of a tripartite climate control skin, which includes insulation and a natural ventilation system. The innovative use of photovoltaic material, energy-efficient heat exchange systems, and recycled materials, in both structural and nonstructural applications, makes the Wall Centre Hotel Vancouver's first "green" skyscraper.

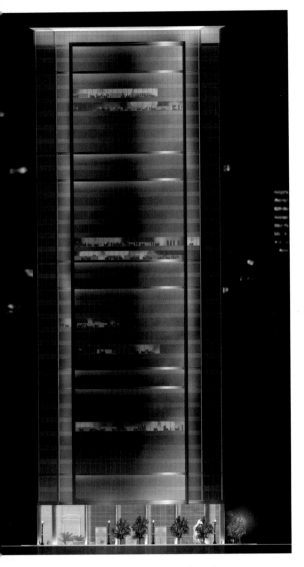

Revised elevation, Dearborn Street

Opposite:
Early draft of the elevation,
One Adams Street

Ground floor plan

Dearborn Center

Architect	Ricardo Bofill, Taller de Arquitectura, Barcelona, Spain
Associate Architect	DeStefano & Partners, Chicago, Illinois, USA
Structural Engineer	TT – CBN/Engineers
Client	Prime/Beitler Development Company, L.L.C.
Location	Chicago, Illinois, USA
Date	Estimated construction 2000 – January 2002

With Chicago's commercial office market only recently recovered from the overbuilding of the 1980s, numerous new office towers have been announced for the downtown business district. For the most part, developers are not yet ready to discuss anchor tenants for their buildings. This is important, since various developers are sitting on more than half a dozen sites around the Loop waiting for tenant commitments to enable the realization of their building plans. However, two large developers have announced construction without substantiated agreements by major tenants: the Dearborn Center and One North Wacker Drive Tower (pp. 24-25). Site preparations and the demolition of existing structures on these lots were already finished in the 1980s, but construction was postponed because of the recession in the 1990s.

In 1998 Chicago developers Prime Group Realty Trust and J. Paul Beitler Development Co. formed a joint venture to build the mixed-use Dearborn Center. Located at a central address in Chicago's Loop and occupying half of a city block bounded by Dearborn Avenue and State and Adams Streets, the building will consist of three basic functional components: below-grade parking, ground level retail, and office floors. The latest plan, redesigned by Barcelona-based Ricardo Bofill of Taller de Arquitectura, is slightly larger than the first one designed by the Chicago firm DeStefano & Partners. At thirty-five stories in height, the Bofill design provides 1,706,585 square feet (158,712 square meters) of retail and office space and accommodates 230 cars on two below-grade levels. Large, open floor-plate office spaces are designed to adapt easily and efficiently to multi-tenant configurations for banks, accounting firms, and trading companies.

Although rising some 567 feet (175 meters), Dearborn Center will not be a major presence in Chicago's skyline. As a result, the building will not have a significant cap or figural top. Instead the design is concentrated on the lower retail section. While the upper levels have a simple aluminum and clear glass curtain wall, the base features detailing typical of Bofill's work, which proved to be successful with the R.R. Donnelley Center in Chicago, another skyscraper designed by Bofill/DeStefano in 1992. At Dearborn Center, the Adams and State Street storefronts, entries, and other special areas will have limestone surfaces in a variety of colors and painted aluminum column covers and cornices—imitating classical architectural forms and elements.

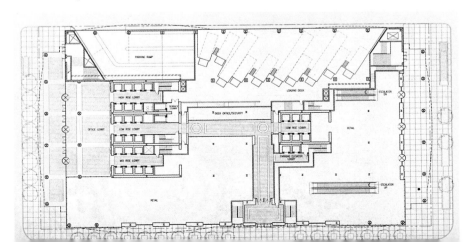

Park Tower

Architect	Lucien Lagrange and Associates, Chicago, Illinois, USA
Structural Engineer	Chris Stefanos Associates
Client	Hyatt Development Corporation
Location	Chicago, Illinois, USA
Date	Estimated construction February 1998 – April 2000

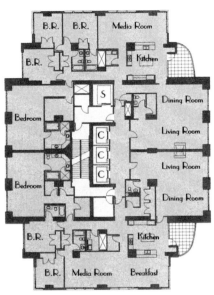

Typical plan

Ground floor plan

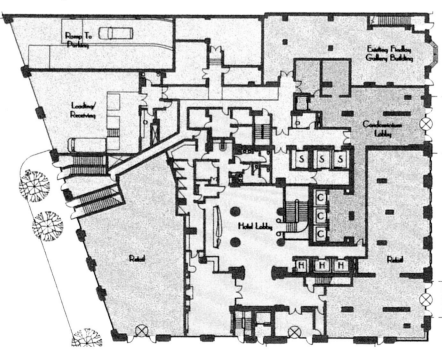

Park Tower replaces the old mid-rise Park Hyatt Hotel whose site proved to be several inches too small for the expanding plans of the new sixty-seven-story hotel and condominium tower. Accordingly, Hyatt was forced to acquire the neighboring Wally Findlay Galleries, a four-story landmark built in 1917. Though the first preference was to keep the entire building, the foundation of the almost 854-foot (260-meter) tall Park Tower required the demolition of the Galleries excluding the protected frontage. A new seven-story structure embraces the remodeled old facade and will house further hotel facilities.

Just across from the historic Water Tower (1869), the mixed-use Park Tower is the first new residential construction along Chicago's Magnificent Mile since the early 1990s. Housing 205 hotel units on floors three through eighteen, and 122 luxury condominiums on the floors above, the stepped back tower is crowned with a pitched copper roof. "The intention is not to look like the Water Tower but to be sympathetic to it," said Hyatt Development Vice President John Lyons in the *Chicago Tribune* (June 30, 1996) to explain the slender tower and the use of rough-finished limestone.

The height of the skyscraper and the site's severe wind conditions led to the installation of one of the world's few specially tuned mass dampers to reduce motion in tall, slender concrete structures. The building will be steadied by a 400-ton, steel-plated weight suspended by a 32-foot (10-meter) cable in its rooftop tower. The weight will work as a pendulum to counterbalance the building's sways in high winds.

Hyatt does not fear any competition from the real estate and hotel boom in down-town Chicago; the developer has announced that nearly fifty percent of the apartments have already been sold, with an average sale price of $1.4 million as recorded by *The New York Times* (March 1, 1998).

Photomontage by
Eric Brightfield (Imagefiction)

One North Wacker Drive

Architect	Lohan Associates, Chicago, Illinois, USA
Structural Engineer	TT – CBM Chicago
Client	John Buck Company/ERE Yarmouth Inc.
Location	Chicago, Illinois, USA
Date	Estimated construction October 1999 – June 2001

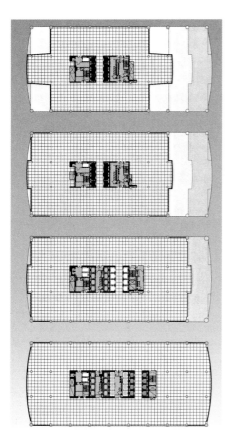

Typical low-rise, mid-rise, first high-rise, and second high-rise floor plans showing step backs

After World War II Chicago underwent a transition from being a predominantly manufacturing center to a service-oriented city. One visible result of the service economy is the growth of skyscrapers in the downtown business center of Chicago. After the boom decade of the 1980s, when skyscrapers were developed as short-term, speculative investments, Chicago, along with much of the rest of the world, entered a period of limited growth. As it enters the new millennium, the city is attempting to revive its reputation as a major service and convention center. Projects for numerous office and hotel towers have been announced, many of them still waiting for major tenants before construction can begin. Site preparations for two projects, the Dearborn Center (pp. 20-21) and One North Wacker Drive, were finished in the 1980s, but construction was postponed until recently because of the recession in the 1990s.

At One North Wacker Drive a commercial office tower is planned by Chicago developer John Buck and Atlanta-based ERE Yarmouth Inc., the latter being a leading U.S. real estate advisor for international investors. Measuring fifty-two stories, the tower will be much taller than the Dearborn Center. Building zoning has been approved by the municipality, and construction is underway. The nearly 650-foot (203-meter) tower will be used entirely for offices, with the exception of some shops on the ground floor and parking facilities below-grade.

James Goettsch, a principal with Lohan Associates who was in charge of Chicago's Blue Cross/Blue Shield Building (pp. 26-27), designed a rectangular glass-and-stainless-steel tower that will be composed of three flat slabs placed next to each other. According to Goettsch's design statement, "the building satisfies the traditional concerns for planning layouts and efficiency and provides the flexibility to accommodate future technologies within an aesthetic that is appropriate for Wacker Drive, the Chicago skyline, and today's business attitudes." Column-free, flexible, open-plan office floors conform to Chicago's requirements for office layouts and work environments, while the glass-and-stainless-steel frame curtain-wall facade recalls the city's architectural traditions and the famed office tower designs of Lohan's grandfather, Mies van der Rohe.

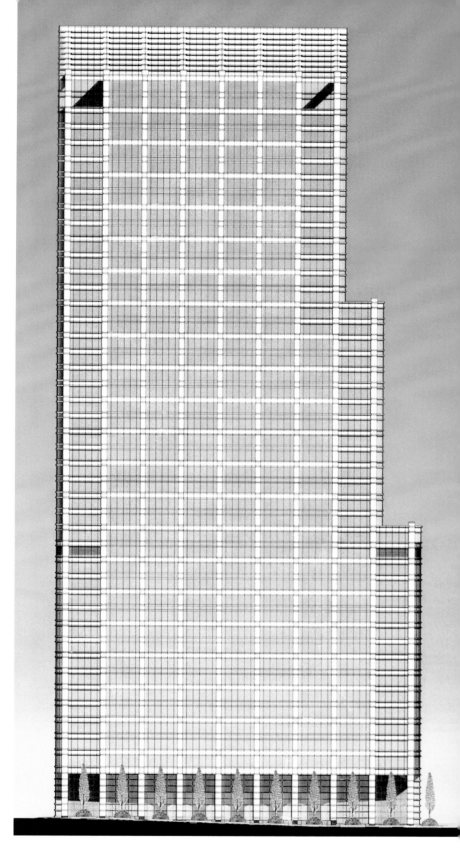

Elevation

View of the lobby

300 East Randolph

Architect	Lohan Associates, Chicago, Illinois, USA
Structural Engineer	Chris Stefanos Associates
Mechanical Engineer	Cosentini Associates
Client	Blue Cross/Blue Shield of Illinois
Location	Chicago, Illinois, USA
Date	Completed 1997

A significant design determinant in early tall office building plans was the requirement to provide natural illumination for the interiors. Therefore, offices were typically designed as a series of interchangeable rooms adjacent to a central light source. However, the introduction of electric light eliminated the real need to design offices as rooms at a building's perimeter. Clearly, offices were conceived as independent units not only as a pragmatic design solution, but also because such a design adequately served the organizational needs of its users. But in the late twentieth century, they were being altered to respond to technologies such as the virtual office and new business philosophies which privilege team or group activities over the traditional hierarchical structure of business management. Consequently, new approaches to design are necessary because the individual office does not always provide the most effective workspace.

Lohan Associates' 300 East Randolph accommodates requirements specific to the Blue Cross/Blue Shield of Illinois organization, the building's only occupant. In response to the client's desire for a functional rather than flashy building, James Goettsch of Lohan Associates designed a simple rectangular building with a stainless steel, aluminum-and-glass clad exterior. The *Chicago Tribune*'s Blair Kamin described the exterior as "verging on the bland" (October 14, 1997), but recognized that such blandness reflected the economic climate of the "Nervous '90s" in which the building was constructed. The building's plan responds to the client's innovative organizational structure and work methods, thus the number of traditional enclosed offices was reduced to less than ten percent of the total work-space. This design permits greater operational flexibility and creates an atmosphere of openness, which reflects the client's desire to reduce the sense of organizational hierarchy.

However, the design of 300 East Randolph is not restricted to its client's current needs. On the contrary, the thirty-story (411 feet or 126.6 meters) modular building was designed to accommodate an additional twenty-four floors for the organization's future growth: a second phase extends the building's height twelve more stories to 567 feet (174 meters), and a third phase extends the building an additional twelve stories to a final height of 731 feet (225 meters). Vertical expansion is possible because the roof is removable, allowing new steel columns to be connected to those directly below, continuing the building's structural design. The increased need for vertical circulation will be served by two more passenger elevator banks, now reserved on the building's north side as a dramatic, vertiginous atrium space adjacent to the two passenger elevator banks now in service.

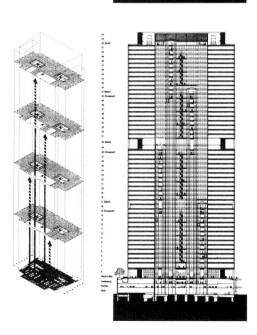

Vertical expansion: phases one and three, east-west section through the atrium showing future growth

Facade

Hotel Sofitel

Architect	Jean-Paul Viguier/s. a. d'architecture, Paris, France
Structural Engineer	Teng & Associates
Client	Accor Sofitel North America
Location	Chicago, Illinois, USA
Date	Estimated construction 1999/2000 – July 2001

Model

Hotel Sofitel in Chicago will be the third luxury hotel in the U. S. besides those in New York and Philadelphia to be opened by Sofitel in the year 2000. The announcement was made in the midst of a hospitality boom in downtown Chicago, where more than thirty hotels providing more than 10,000 future hotel rooms are being developed, redeveloped, or planned because of Chicago's longtime presence as one of America's most important convention centers. Located at a prime Gold Coast site, the new Sofitel Hotel (412 rooms) will compete with ventures from major chains such as Hyatt (220 rooms), Hilton (350 rooms), and the developer Richard Stein (396 rooms), within the space of a few blocks. John Lehody, President of Accor North America, explained in the *Chicago Tribune* that "overbuilding has been the story of the hotel industry" (March 25, 1998), and that the plans of other hotels will not deter his company, which operates one of the world's largest hotel networks with more than

2,500 hotels in about seventy countries. He calculates that due to the strong demand in Chicago, the market can easily absorb 6,000 of the planned rooms.

According to Jean-Paul Viguier's design statement, his major concern is to "establish a volumetric composition which articulates the horizontal elements for the public spaces and the vertical elements for the private spaces, a structured geometry in a contemporary French classical tradition." To realize this vision, he has stacked twenty-seven stories of guest rooms on top of three floors of public spaces and reception areas. The prismatic tower is connected to an elliptically shaped plaza located at the rear where it is protected from vehicular traffic. The tower, defined by alternating, horizontal layers of glass and polished white stone, smoothly projects out from the site boundary creating an "emblematic figure" that stands out from the usual block-like infills in Chicago's urban grid.

Projected view
from street level

Photomontage
showing urban
context

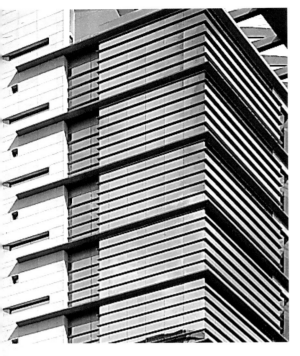

Facade detail

Portland Federal Courthouse

Architect	Kohn Pedersen Fox Associates, P. C., New York, New York, USA
Structural Engineer	KPFF Engineering
Client	U.S. General Services Administration
Location	Portland, Oregon, USA
Date	Completed 1997

Even if the skyscraper is most commonly associated with commercial use, it is nevertheless a flexible building type, as Kohn Pedersen Fox's sixteen-story courthouse in Portland demonstrates. Providing 602,000 square feet (55,926 square meters) of space, the building proved an ideal form in which to house the city's court and its related agencies.

The firm's design was generated by a desire to express the building's civic function. While both the bureaucratic and judicial sections are maintained in a single structure, the firm clarified the building's complex program by visually distinguishing the judicial areas from the bureaucratic ones. From the exterior, the building's various functions are articulated by its massing. Such distinctions are reinforced by the use of different materials.

The sections of the building that contain courtrooms are clad in traditional materials such as granite and limestone to symbolically express the weighty significance of such a function in a democratic society. In contrast, the sections of the building that are both literally and metaphorically more open to the public, such as the circulation galleries and the judges' chambers, are constructed of visually lighter materials such as aluminum, stainless steel, and reflective glass. The building's design also engages the local landscape. Inspired by the shape of a sail, the building's roof, for example, responds to both the Wilamette River and Mount Hood in the distance.

Two views
showing the building's
multifaceted character

Westin New York
at Times Square/E Walk

Architect	Arquitectonica, Miami, Florida, USA
Structural Engineer	Cantor Seinuk Group, P. C.
Client	Tishman Realty & Construction Company, Incorporated
Location	Times Square, New York, New York, USA
Date	Estimated construction 2000 – 2002

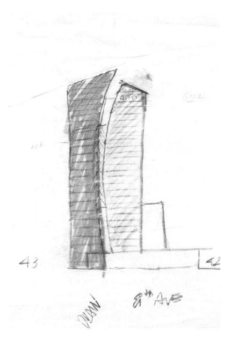

Conceptual drawing by Laurinda Spear

Opposite:
Revised model of the project in the cityscape
by Re. PRESENTATION, Incorporated

Detail of a computer-generated model

In a press conference in May 1995, New York Governor George Pataki and New York City Mayor Rudolph W. Giuliani announced Arquitectonica's E Walk ("Entertainment Walk") as the winning design for the New York Urban Development Corporation's (UDC) revitalization project for the area bounded by 42nd and 43rd Streets and 7th and 8th Avenues. The 42nd Street urban renewal program is one of the most extensive in the country. Created by New York architect Robert A. M. Stern, the UDC's urban design guidelines dictate a lower retail podium along 42nd Street, an intermediate section at the corner of 42nd Street and 8th Avenue, and a recessed tower at the corner of 43rd Street and 8th Avenue. These guidelines also set the criteria for signage on both a building's base and top. Even though the guidelines themselves have not been the target of extensive criticism, the Times Square renovation has resulted in controversy. In particular, protesters charge that revitalization efforts replace the "real" New York with an artificial, sanitized version.

But according to Herbert Muschamp in *The New York Times*, Arquitectonica's project "capture[s] the spirit of place" with its "unsubtle fusion of erotics and economics that is Times Square" (May 21, 1995). Even so, Arquitectonica states that their design solution does not strictly and stylistically continue the traditional 1930s New York setback skyscraper, but instead "move[s] forward to a next generation." Consequently, what could be interpreted as a traditional skyscraper has been reconfigured specifically to Westin New York/E Walk's program. The base is a retail podium, whose large-scale advertisements evoke the tradition of the Times Square billboard. Above this rises the tower of the Westin Hotel, two forty-five-story prisms offering 860 rooms as well as conference space.

The various sections of the skyscraper take on different meanings depending on the viewer's position. Its irregular profile can be read as either a "rock" upon which the tower rests or as a "meteor" that has split the tower in two. Likewise, the effect of the building changes according to whether one views its profile from the east, when its horizontal pattern of back-painted glass in celadon, gold, and rust is visible, or from the west, when the bands of steel and blue-gray glass that emphasize the form's verticality may be seen. Yet regardless of the building's shifting meanings, its emphatic movement upward presents an appropriate effect for a skyscraper.

LVMH Tower

Architect	Atelier Christian de Portzamparc, Paris, France
Structural Engineer	Weiskops and Pickworth
Client	Louis Vuitton Moët Hennessy Group
Location	New York, New York, USA
Date	Completed 1999

French architect Christian de Portzamparc's tower for the American headquarters of Louis Vuitton, the luggage manufacturer, is an architectural expression of the new profile of one of most extensive luxury goods empires in the world. As Bernard Arnoult, chairman of LVMH, attempts to explore new commercial territories with Vuitton's first line of prêt-à-porter fashion and to change the firm's product promotion to be more glamorous and Hollywood-esque, so the LVMH Tower is an attempt at new architectural forms and expressions.

The building is located on an extremely narrow site between two high rises on 57th Street between Fifth and Madison Avenues. The facade of the twenty-three-story tower conforms precisely to the setbacks prescribed in the city's building regulation code. The body of the tower breaks up into interlocking irregular volumes and shapes, including a significant step back above the tenth floor. Like a giant lily, the front facade opens up like petals, revealing the "heart of the flower," according to Portzamparc in *The New York Times* (November 8, 1996).

The exterior is clad in alternating clear and opalescent glass, while the flower's heart is sheathed in blue, crystalline glass. The building's slender, prismatic shell accentuates the structure beneath it, and reflects Portzamparc's concept that a building requires an organic relationship between structure, site, and facade. The plastic

expression of the building is emphasized at night, when concealed neon lights tint the facade with a palette of soft colors and white lights illuminate the underside of the floor slabs.

While the exterior is nonlinear and somewhat erratic, the interior follows a simple, column-free floor plan featuring a completely glazed facade that offers not only natural daylight but also extensive views of the New York cityscape.

Opposite:
Early study models
for design

Photomontage of view from street level

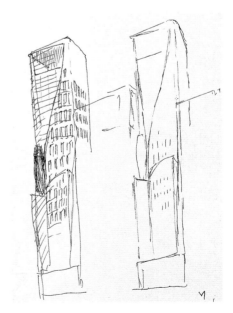

Preliminary sketch

Under construction, March 1999

Low-rise floor plan

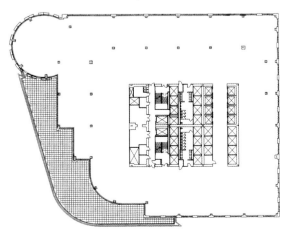

The Condé Nast Building
at Four Times Square

Architect	Fox & Fowle Architects, P. C., New York, New York, USA
Structural Engineer	Canton Seinuk Group, P. C.
Client	The Durst Organization
Location	New York, New York, USA
Date	Completion expected 1999

Situated on the northeast corner of Broadway and 42nd Street, the Condé Nast Building is the first speculative office building to be constructed as part of the 42nd Street Development's large-scale revitalization program of Times Square. Other new Times Square skyscrapers include Fox & Fowle's Reuters Building at Three Times Square and Arquitectonica's E Walk on 42nd Street.

Fox & Fowle was selected in 1995 by the New York City Department of General Services as one of only four architectural firms qualified to design "green" projects for New York City. Behind their design for the Condé Nast building was a commitment to minimizing the fourty-eight-story tower's impact on the surrounding environment, as specially requested by the client. Fox & Fowle employed several strategies in their effort to achieve contextual sensitivity. In *The New York Times* Herbert Muschamp praised one in particular: the building's scale. Unlike an earlier design by Philip Johnson and John Burgee for the same site, Muschamp wrote that Fox & Fowle's project "will be far less catastrophic. . ." [since] ". . . it is not monstrously out of scale with the parade of new towers that have arisen on Broadway in recent years" (May 18, 1996).

The use of two different facades, each of which relates to two different environments, is another means by which Fox & Fowle conformed the new skyscraper to existing conditions. The western facade is a metal and glass curtain wall punctuated by billboards at the pedestrian level which reflect the pop culture sensibility historically associated with Times Square. By contrast, the eastern facade is masonry, which coexists harmoniously with the elegant environs of Bryant Park.

Fox & Fowle's commitment to sustainable architecture is especially evident in the Condé Nast Building's interior, which maximizes feasible sources of natural light and energy with "green" features such as energy-creating photovoltaic cells, an automatic lighting program prompted by natural light conditions, and an energy-efficient climate control system that functions in conjunction with the wastewater system to cool the offices while also minimizing fossil fuel usage. Moreover, all of the products used in the building's interior design were selected because of their minimal impact on interior and exterior air quality as well as their high standard of sustainability and recyclability.

An outstanding aspect of the interior of the building is a fourth-floor, 260-seat cafeteria—featuring blue titanium, ash veneer, and stainless steel—designed by Frank O. Gehry. The main dining room has booths distributed along the perimeter and tables enclosed by curved glass panels in the center, creating an atmosphere that is both open and intimate.

View from
mid-rise
vantage point

Ironically, considering the architects' efforts
at reducing the environmental impact of the
Condé Nast Building, the building's construction has had its problems. In January of
1998, a crane carrying several tons of granite
struck a neighboring building, releasing
bricks and posing a great danger to passing
pedestrians. More seriously, a scaffolding
collapsed on July 21, 1998 resulting in the
death of an eighty-five-year-old woman,
indicating that dangers still exist when con-
structing tall buildings in dense urban areas.

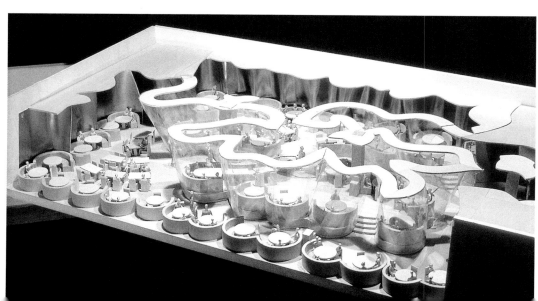

Cafeteria designed
by Frank O. Gehry
& Associates

The Reuters Building

Architect	Fox & Fowle Architects, P. C., New York, New York, USA
Structural Engineer	Severud Associates
Client	Three Times Square Associates, LLC
Location	New York, New York, USA
Date	Completion expected 2001

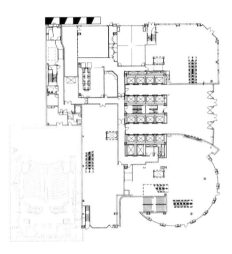

Ground floor plan

The New York City Times Square revitalization project has been controversial. One issue in particular—city and state corporate tax exemptions—has received a significant amount of attention. In an article for *The New York Times* (November 1, 1997), Charles V. Bagli reported that Reuters American Holdings received tax breaks worth more than $60 million in exchange for constructing a new headquarters in Times Square. State Senator Franz Leichter's critique of Mayor Rudolph W. Giuliani's effort is characteristic: "Giuliani has made Times Square the tax break or corporate welfare of the world."

In contrast to Senator Leichter's comments, which imply that the Reuters Building is not a good neighbor, *The New York Times'* Herbert Muschamp has described Fox & Fowle's design as "decent, well mannered and deferential," adding that "if you were a gentleman, you would tip your hat" (March 8, 1998).

The design problem posed by Fox & Fowle's Reuters Building is not unlike that of their earlier skyscraper, the Condé Nast Building. Located near one another in Times Square, both towers incorporate differently designed facades that blend into their existing contexts, a strategy that Muschamp has praised as "one of the strengths of buildings designed by Fox & Fowle" (May 18, 1996). Yet in contrast to the Condé Nast Building, the Reuters Building is designed to be a more emphatic corporate symbol, which is not surprising since the design of the Condé Nast Building was, as Muschamp has observed, "largely completed before Condé Nast decided to be the building's main tenant" (May 18, 1996). The refined, curved surface of the thirty-story eastern facade symbolizes Reuters' corporate identity on a large scale while the company's presence is reasserted more specifically at several different levels on the building's other facades. These include a dynamic, illuminated, wedge-shaped sign that penetrates the glazing on the building's eastern side—a large cylindrical, electronic, display described as "spectacular," that rises fourteen stories through the center of the building's northeast corner—and a series of

zipper signs relaying Reuters' news and financial information at the pedestrian level on the eastern side.

The visual impact of the expansive glass curtain wall on the building's eastern side is reduced on the other sides by relating the massing to adjacent buildings like the New Victory Theater on its southern side. In contrast to the reflective glazing used for the eastern elevation, the other facades are clad in stone and terra-cotta. The contrasting southern and eastern facades are connected by a drum-shaped rotunda that serves as the tower's entrance. The inclusion of large-scale signage above the rotunda ties the Reuters Building to not only the decorative traditions of specific buildings but also to the commercial pastiche historically associated with Times Square.

Left and right:
The building as a support
for large scale signage

The Impala Building

Architect	Michael Graves & Associates, Princeton, New Jersey, USA
Associate Architect	H. Thomas O'Hara
Structural Engineer	DeSimone Consulting Engineers
Client	RFR Davis & Partners, L. P.
Location	New York, New York, USA
Date	Completion expected 2000

Located at the corner of 1st Avenue and 76th Street in Manhattan, the Impala Building consists of a seven-story base and a twenty-four-story tower. While a mixed-use program is hardly unique in the modern skyscraper, the Impala Building's combination of commercial, retail, and residential spaces results from specific zoning restrictions that required the greater part of the site to be reserved strictly for residential use. The section of the building facing 1st Avenue will contain commercial and retail space, while medical offices will occupy the section facing 76th Street. Housing will be inserted into the 75th Street base as well as the tower. The 260,000-square-foot (24,154-square-meter) rental apartment complex will contain 189 units in three buildings around a landscaped courtyard with a pool.

Known as one of the first major American architects to promote contextually sensitive architecture, Michael Graves designed the Impala Building to reference the traditional residential buildings on New York City's upper East Side. Primarily constructed of brick and stone, its neo-Georgian facade is particularly reminiscent of the city's historic buildings. However, the large scale of the Impala Building has required certain modifications in order to maintain proper proportions—such as the visual compression of two stories into one through the use of double-height, precast frames around the windows.

Detail of the
1st Avenue elevation
at street level

Perspective from the
corner of 1st Avenue
and 71st Street

Glazed entry from
interior and exterior

350 Madison Avenue

Architect	Skidmore, Owings & Merrill LLP, New York, New York, USA
Structural Engineer	Gilsanz, Murray Steficek
Client	Max Capital Management
Location	New York, New York, USA
Date	Completion expected September 2001

The New York office of Skidmore, Owings & Merrill is famed for its modernist steel-and-glass skyscrapers such as the Lever Brothers Company Office Building (1951–52) in New York City. The commission to renovate and add to an existing twenty-four-story office building from the 1920s at 350 Madison Avenue provided an opportunity for the firm to consider the tall building type from another design perspective.

The client's program required a new lobby at street level and approximately 50,000 square feet (4,645 square meters) of new office space added above the existing building. Rather than design an addition that would be undifferentiated from the original brick building, Skidmore, Owings & Merrill created a dramatic addition constructed of frosted glass, stainless steel mesh, and polished concrete that enlivens the older structure. A new glass storefront will unify a retail store with the lobby at the base, while a partial over-cladding of the tower will connect the lobby with the roof. Also, the building's original dark entrance will be transformed into a brightly illuminated space. The lobby floor and ceiling will be constructed entirely of glass, and floodlights will be mounted beneath the lobby floor and directed upward where they will reflect off of the new metal mesh surface of the south face of the building. Herbert Muschamp of *The New York Times* enthusiastically described designer Roger Duffy's solution as one that "turns the wheel . . . heavenly stuff . . . an embryonic building type: an innovative approach to building vertically in an already built-up city" (May 16, 1999).

Model showing
overall massing

Computer-generated
images of the atrium
and the plaza
by Carlos Diniz

Bird's-eye view of building massing

Torre Mayor

Architect	Zeidler Roberts Partnership, Toronto, Canada
Associate Architect	Adamson Associates Architects
Structural Engineer	The Cantor Seinuk Group
Client	ICA Reichmann Torre Mayor
Location	Mexico City, Mexico
Date	Estimated construction Fall 1997 – Fall 2002

The Torre Mayor rises 738 feet (226 meters) and will be the tallest building in Latin America. A building of this height in Mexico City faces major challenges, namely overcoming the wet, jelly-like clay soil and fulfilling seismic requirements in one of the most active earthquake areas in the world. For this reason, Torre Mayor has been designed to float, carefully balancing the above and below ground masses of the building components. The foundation of the tower is a combined pile-mat system, with piles that are connected by a reinforced concrete raft supporting the building's load on the hard layer of Mexico City's bedrock. To provide flexibility in the case of an earthquake, a system of pistons, three feet in diameter, placed at the intersections of the diagonal bracing along the perimeter of the tower has been invented to simultaneously dampen the dynamic loads and maintain the integrity of the facade.

The fifty-five-story tower juxtaposes two basic geometric forms: a cylinder and a rectangle. The rectangular tower is encased in pinkish-red granite, perforated in a uniform pattern by office windows. The curved facade, on the other hand, consists of double-glazed, lightly tinted glass panels and spandrels. The stone tower ends below a mechanical penthouse, exposing the sharp-edged top of the glass tower. The glass tower's mullions create a second and third grid over the initial mullion pattern, thus creating a net-like tension over its surface. The curvature of the semi-transparent glass body serves two goals: to avoid the reflections of adjacent buildings and to mirror the gentle bending of the Paseo de la Reforma, the 325-foot (100-meter) wide avenue that runs in front of the Torre Mayor. Both architect and client believe that the "the design—with its elegant play between stone and glass, rectangular and curvilinear form—will not only create an efficient office building but also a powerful, marketable image in the urban context of Mexico City."

A two-story podium housing 34,445 square feet (3,200 square meters) of shops and restaurants sits below the tower with two wings meeting the street line. They are meant to mediate between the enormous height of the tower and the neighboring two-story buildings on either side, as well as shelter an open plaza from the heavy traffic of the Paseo.

Photomontage of the tower
in Mexico City's skyline

View from street level

Torre Paris Corporate Headquarters

Architect	Loebl Schlossman & Hackl, Chicago, Illinois, USA
Associate Architect	Jaime Bendersky e Asociados
Structural Engineer	Arze, Recine y Asociados
Client	Senior Juan Galmez Couso
Location	Santiago, Chile
Date	Completed 1999

In the early 1990s, an economic recession suspended building activity in the United States. As a result, many American architectural firms expanded into the international market. As Margaret Littman observed in *Crain's Chicago Business*: "International work has long been a means for U.S. firms to cushion themselves against the cyclical nature of the domestic real estate industry" (March 23, 1998). In the first half of the 1990s, Asia was the dominant foreign market for American architects. In fact, Cesar Pelli's Petronas Towers in Malaysia (pp. 82-83)—capturing the title of "World's Tallest Building"—symbolize the impact of American architectural design on the built environment in Asia.

While the importance of the Asian market cannot be ignored, other regions have also provided American architectural firms with opportunities to build. In Latin America, Chile was considered the area's economic bastion in the early 1990s. Described as an "economic jaguar," its free-market model was first implemented under General Augusto Pinochet's dictatorship in the early 1970s. Even though Pinochet's military actions have been strongly criticized both domestically and internationally, a recent article in *The New York Times* stated that "Many Chileans …applaud the military government's pro-market economic policies, which they credit

with bringing Chile prosperity" (March 11, 1998). It was Chile's new economic environment that encouraged American architecture firms like Chicago-based Loebl Schlossman & Hackl to develop their practices there. In early 1998, the firm's president—Donald J. Hackl—maintained his confidence in the country, even though the Asian economic crisis also had substantial repercussions there. To boost investor confidence, the Chilean government has recently decreased federal spending, while also reducing constraints on foreign investment.

Loebl Schlossman & Hackl's first Chilean commission is a twenty-two-story corporate headquarters with commercial and office space for Almacenes Paris, a local department store chain founded by the prominent Galmez family. The building was commissioned to celebrate the 100th year anniversary of the family's arrival in Chile and their retail success. However, for the local community, the modern Torre Paris building also symbolizes the future of Santiago. The reinforced steel frame structure incorporates metal coated glass of various colors and granite in a series of "layered planes" which respond to programmatic requirements as well as define elevations and massing in relation to the site and the surrounding buildings. When completed the tower will provide flexible, column-free office floors with spectacular views of the city and its environment.

Project rendering

ANTEL Telecommunications Tower

Architect	Carlos Ott International, Montevideo, Uruguay
Structural Engineer	Marcelo Sasson
Client	Adminstracion Nacional de Telecomunicaciones
Location	Montevideo, Uruguay
Date	Estimated construction April 1997 – December 2000

Situated on a prominent site overlooking the harbor of Montevideo, the new headquarters of the publicly owned national telecommunications agency of Uruguay, ANTEL, is intended to represent a bold architectural expression of the company's progressive and successful role in Latin America's telecommunications market. Over the past two years, ANTEL has converted to a fully digital system that satisfies the country's telecommunications needs and enables company expansion through Latin American joint ventures. The new ANTEL Telecommunications Tower is a symbol of its contemporary and prosperous corporate identity, especially since it incorporates the latest advancements in computer, telecommunications, security, and environmental control systems. The tower, 520 feet (160 meters) high including the antenna, is an irregular juxtaposition of triangular and curved volumes of differing heights. Thirty of its occupied floors contain both public and corporate spaces, while the top floors house the ANTEL antenna, leaving additional space for other private telecommunications antennas.

The ANTEL headquarters complex is also composed of several low-rise structures, including a curvilinear building adjacent to the tower that contains client facilities and an irregular block on the opposite side that houses an amphitheater, day-care center, and parking garage. Nearby, an inverted conical structure and connected triangular building serve as a telecommunications museum and multi-functional hall. The irregular geometry and asymmetrical arrangement of the buildings contrasts with the orthogonal street grid and site boundaries. The irregular and shifting facades as well as the alternating black-and-gray granite exterior cladding, tri-colored aluminum curtain wall, and green, blue-green, and silver glass all contribute to the dynamic expression of the ANTEL Telecommunications Tower.

View of the model

Governor Philip Tower
Governor Macquarie Tower

Architect	Denton Corker Marshall, Sydney, Australia
Structural Engineer	Ove Arup & Partners
Clients	State Authorities Superannuation Board
	Now Morgan Grenfell Ltd. (Australia)
Location	Sydney, Australia
Date	Governor Philip Tower completed 1993
	Governor Macquarie Tower completed 1994

View of the GPT foyer

In the early 1990s, two large development complexes were built by Denton Corker Marshall (DCM) and Renzo Piano (pp. 50-51) as part of a vast program by the Australian government to reconstruct Sydney's business center. In 1989 DCM was commissioned to design the sixty-four-story Governor Philip Tower (GPT), the forty-six-story Governor Macquarie Tower (GMT), Governors' Place, and the Museum of Sydney. A major task for the architects involved was to reconcile the great need for office space and the height of the towers with the difficult archaeological requirements of the site.

The towers were to be built on the site of the earliest British colony in Australia. Thus, the municipality requested that the architects preserve and integrate the ruins of the first Government House, which occupied the area from 1788 until its demolition in 1852. In DCM's winning design the footings of the house are conserved in situ, their outlines marked on the paving through a change of texture and materials. The Museum of Sydney was built adjacent to Governor's Place to exhibit the artifacts found during excavation. The predominant use of local sandstone—in varying textures, sizes, and surface finishes—for the three-story museum expresses the archaeological layers of the site and its surrounding historical district.

The municipality further insisted on the preservation of two rows of nineteenth century Victorian terrace houses. Because space had to be left above these houses, the GPT was built on a series of twenty-story columns, each supporting massive cross beams which cantilever some twenty-six feet (eight meters) over residential backyards. These beams visually separate the rectangular curtain-wall tower from its sandstone base, shared with the other tower, where an entrance hall and three lobbies are located.

Compared to the richness of materials and details in the lower public levels, the main bodies of the towers appear rigid and subdued. Designed on horizontal and vertical grids, they are clad in polished granite and gray zinc, inspired by the zinc roofs of nearby historic buildings. Vertical mullions are the only three-dimensional elaboration of the facade. In fact, the prismatic towers repeat basic principles of modernist functionalism: regular forms, repetitive window patterns, and uniform colors and materials. This is because the architect Barry Marshall wanted the buildings to be understood as a "sculptural abstract" complex.

The two towers might have entered into a contextual dialogue with the North-South Wales Government Headquarters—called the

Aerial view
of both towers:
GPT, left,
and GMT, right

Bottom right:
Site plan

State Office Block—directly across Macquarie
Street, but that building was demolished in
1996 to make way for the 155 Macquarie
Street development designed by Renzo Piano
(pp. 50-51).

View of the GMT from street level

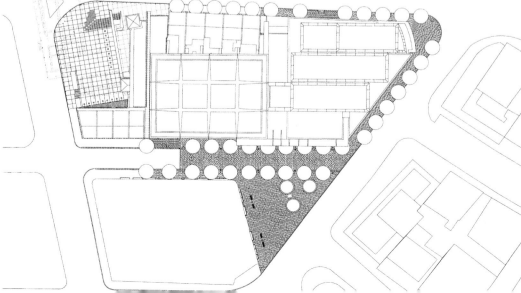

Model of the complex including projects by Denton Corker Marshall

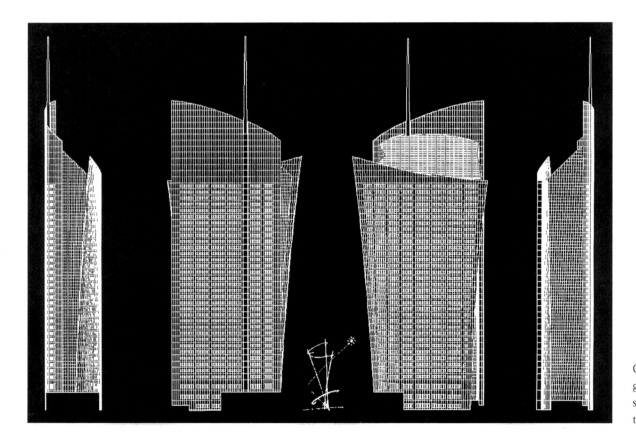

Computer-
generated
study of the
tower's form

155 Macquarie Street Tower

Architect	Renzo Piano Building Workshop, Genoa, Italy
Structural Engineer	Ove Arup & Partners
Client	Lend Lease Development
Location	Sydney, Australia
Date	Estimated construction January 1998 – October 2000

The construction of Renzo Piano's 155 Macquarie Street Residential Building & Commercial Tower Complex in Sydney provoked controversy because it included the demolition of the State Office Block, by Ken Wooley, erected on the site in 1976. Although Wooley's building was considered to be one of the first modern icons in Australia, it was eventually torn down in order to make way for the significant boost in commercial activities and construction related to the approaching Olympics 2000 in Sydney. Its replacement, by Piano, is composed of a thirty-four-story office tower and a sixteen-story apartment block linked by a public plaza beneath a transparent glass canopy that is suspended by steel cables between the two towers.

According to Piano, three key factors were important in designing the complex: "environment, historical context, and social life." His "non-hermetic towers" respond sensitively to the built and natural environment and create interactive relationships between the historic district, the nearby Royal Botanical Gardens, and the bay. The residential tower will be among the most prestigious and luxurious in the city, with each of its sixty-two apartments having its own glass-louvered balcony providing panoramic views of the harbor and the Botanical Gardens. The office tower, with its two huge sails of sintered glass wrapped around a conventional concrete structure, will pay tribute in form and shimmering material to Jørn Utzon's

famous Opera House (1957–73) only 2,600 feet (800 meters) away. Additionally, the tower's corners, where the elliptical core is exposed, are covered with terra-cotta panels whose color and texture is similar to Sydney's native, yellow sandstone.

Instead of getting smaller as it rises like many other towers, the upper floors of the 155 Macquarie Street Tower cantilever outwards on the northeastern side, terminating in a shell-shaped roof that incorporates a communications tower above the western facade. Upon its completion in the year 2000, the office tower will stand as an expressive landmark on Sydney's skyline.

Top and right: Elevations showing two different views of the site

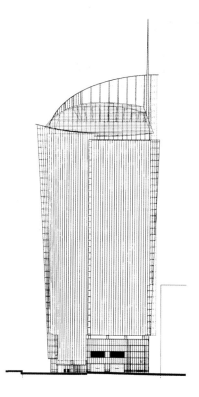

Aerial view

Opposite: View of the lobby

View of the tower dominating Hong Kong's skyline

Computer rendering of the atrium interior

The Center

Architect   Dennis Lau & Ng Chun Man Architects + Engineers
(H. K.) Ltd, Hong Kong, People's Republic of China
Structural Engineer   Maunsell Consultant Asia Ltd
Clients   Land Development Corporation
Cheung Kong (Holdings) Ltd
Location   Hong Kong, People's Republic of China
Date   Completed 1998

Despite many doubts, the construction boom in Hong Kong has continued after the city was handed over to the People's Republic of China. While building activities in the 1970s and 1980s were concentrated in new cities in the hinterland, new skyscrapers now soar in the highly congested central business district of Hong Kong. However, a consequence of the Asian economic crisis and crash of real estate prices is that even highrise projects in prime downtown locations—with luxurious facades of highly polished granite and reflective glass—often have to wait for tenants and buyers.

An architectural response to this cycle of boom and bust is exemplified in The Center, by Dennis Lau & Ng Chun Man, and Olympia Plaza, by Wong Tung & Partners (pp. 54-55), both developed by renowned Hong Kong architectural firms. Located in the dynamic business center of Hong Kong Island, both skyscrapers offer attractive facades designed to draw pedestrians into their retail stores, making the buildings desirable to commercial tenants, and, to lower building costs, both maximize every inch of the gross floor area possible from the relatively limited building sites.

The Center shoots up some 1,125 feet (346 meters), including its antenna, making it a prominent feature of Hong Kong's skyline. Rising above neighboring buildings,

The Center attracts attention with reflective glass and dramatic illumination. Its seventy-three office floors are raised almost forty-nine feet (fifteen meters) above ground to create space for a landscaped plaza and generous entrance lobby. By incorporating this open atrium into his building, Dennis Lau claims to have inserted "breathing space" into the existing chaotic traffic.

The Center's exterior has a regular pattern of rectangular blocks and projecting triangular bays that create twice the number of income-producing corner offices. The top floors step back into a slender pyramid, resembling an earlier building by Dennis Lau & Ng Chun Man, the triangular Central Plaza from 1992 which rises 1,232 feet (379 meters), including its antenna, and was considered the world's tallest reinforced concrete structure for years.

Olympia Plaza

Architect	Wong Tung & Partners, Hong Kong, People's Republic of China
Structural Engineer	Joseph Chow & Partners Ltd.
Client	Ka Chee Co. Ltd.
Location	Hong Kong, People's Republic of China
Date	Completed 1999

Curvilinear suspended glass enclosure for elevators

In contrast to The Center (pp. 52-53), which is a slender and soaring landmark on Hong Kong's skyline, Olympia Plaza is only twenty-six stories high and rises only some 387 feet (119 meters). Occupying the narrow end of a block in the city's commercial district, the building is exposed to three streets that have heavy vehicular and pedestrian traffic. Because its rooftop is not visible within the city skyline, the tower's design concentrates on the lower levels, which are more obvious to potential customers.

The building design follows a tripartite scheme in terms of both function and appearance. The mixed commercial use of the building is clearly revealed in the form and arrangement of its facade: three podium levels are used as shopping arcades, above which are eight middle levels for restaurants and kitchen areas, topped by fourteen floors of offices.

To attract pedestrians into the retail podium, Olympia Plaza's exterior is divided into a grid of metal light boxes displaying banners and advertisements. Also, two column-free transparent cylinders are cut into the corners of the rectangular podium and function as display windows. Accentuating their profile are glass blocks which serve as beacons at night.

The middle levels are recessed from the site boundary with clear, floor-to-ceiling windows which offer extensive views into and out of the restaurants. Three elevators rise in transparent glass tubes along the mid-levels facing King's Road and are echoed by two triangular structures on the opposite elevation.

The office floors project over the mid-levels, forming a convex facade. Linear trim along the silver, reflective curtain wall emphasizes the horizontal breadth of the building—a design feature that is reiterated even in the horizontal bands around the glass cylinders and elevator enclosures—and compresses vertical movement. This underlines the architect's intention, according to his statement in The Pace (October 1997), to give the overall composition a "coherent and dynamic form," which emphasizes the "streamlined" qualities of "horizontality and transparency."

Although the design of Olympia Plaza is intended to attract customers and stimulate consumption, the success of the project is endangered by increasing unemployment and impoverishment in Hong Kong as well as by the declining number of consumer-oriented tourists.

Tripartite composition:
retail base,
transparent restaurants,
and office tower

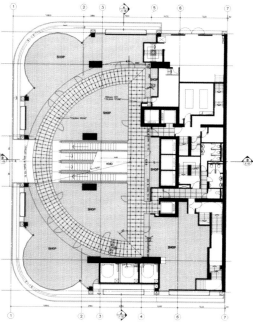

First-floor plan

Site plan in urban context

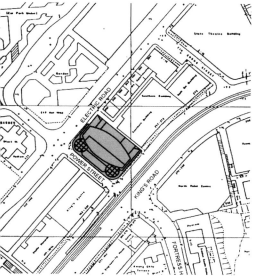

Shanghai Information Town

Architect	Arquitectonica, Miami, Florida, USA
Structural Engineer	East China Architectural Design & Research Institute
Client	Shanghai Information Town Development Company
Location	Shanghai, People's Republic of China
Date	Smaller tower completed 1998; completion of larger tower expected 2002

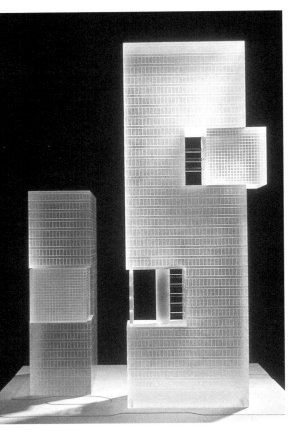

Model by Re. PRESENTATION, Incorporated

In the first half of the 1990s, China experienced economic growth at double-digit rates. But, like other emerging markets in Asia, China's economy slowed by the second half of the decade. Regardless, the Chinese government remains committed to the construction industry as an important factor in the country's economic development. The government's desire to continue the country's construction boom is encouraged by what *Architectural Record* characterized as "a shortage of retail and commercial space in China's larger cities. . . ." (July 1994). These mixed-use projects are generally high-profile and designed by foreign architects. One such example is Arquitectonica's Shanghai Information Town.

Its steel-and-glass towers are simple rectangular forms, reflective of the firm's Modernist sensibility. However—in contrast to High Modernist skyscrapers—two square sections of the twenty-five and fifty story buildings are cantilevered from the buildings' cores, visually destabilizing the otherwise static, rectangular forms. The bottom half of the fifty-story tower is also punctuated by a square void, which is defined by the tower's wall on one side and by a square screen on the other. The architectonic void, famously demonstrated in the design of the Miami condominium Atlantis, is an Arquitectonica signature.

The towers are arranged at right angles, exploiting the dramatic relationship between the sliding cube of the twenty-five-story tower and the screened cubic void of the fifty-story tower. Nonetheless, the distinctive forms of the two towers are not as idiosyncratic as they first appear: the shorter tower repeats the design of the upper section of the taller one, and both adhere to the same 20,000-square foot floor plan (1,859 square meters). The seeming complexity of the towers' design is thereby created with a minimum of architectonic means.

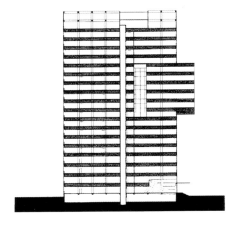

Section

Perspective view

Grand Gateway at Xu Jia Hui

Architect	Callison Architecture, Seattle, Washington, USA
Associate Architect	Frank C. Y. Feng Architects and Associates, (HK) Ltd.
Structural Engineer	Maunsell Consultant Asia Ltd
Clients	Hang Lung Development Co. Ltd.
	Henderson Land Development
	Hysan Development Co. Ltd.
	Xuhui Property Development Co. Ltd.
Location	Shanghai, People's Republic of China
Date	Phase 1 completed 1999

Offering more than 3.3 million square feet (306,900 square meters) of gross floor area, the Grand Gateway by Callison Architecture is one of China's largest development projects. Competing with burgeoning development in the Pudong area (see pp. 62-71), this project is planned as a distinctive gateway to Xu Jia Hui, another rapidly developing commercial district of Shanghai. Enormous streams of visitors are expected because the site is connected to the city's largest and busiest subway station.

The entire project consists of two fifty-two-story towers, separated by a six-story retail and entertainment complex, and four towers of varying heights towards the rear. The complex is composed of cubical and cylindrical geometric forms. The two identical office towers are intended to function as a symbolic portal to the new development. Giant video screens accentuate the entrance into the podium where themed retail environments imitate the ambiance of Paris, Hollywood, and traditional Chinese settings. While the interiors were intended by Callison Architecture to create a "nonstop living theater for visitors to see and to be seen in," the exterior is defined by a rigid and repetitive grid of windows. The towers' facades follow a set-back scheme to reduce mass and emphasize verticality.

Realization of the gigantic project began in 1994 with two luxury residential towers surrounded by landscaped areas. While these two towers have been completed, the retail complex and office towers suffer from the oversupply of office space, as a result of the construction boom in Shanghai. Therefore, construction of Phase II, the office towers and retail sections, has been postponed.

Residential tower

Computer-generated
image of the 'gateway'

Section of the retail
and entertainment complex

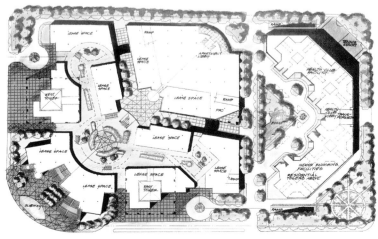

Site plan

Wan Xiang International Plaza

Architect	Ingenhoven Overdiek und Partner, Düsseldorf, Germany
Associate Architect	East China Architectural Design and Research Institute
Structural Engineer	Buro Happold
Client	Shanghai Wan Xiang International Plaza Co. Ltd.
Location	Shanghai, People's Republic of China
Date	Estimated construction October 1999 – January 2003

In 1995 the well-known German firm Ingenhoven Overdiek und Partner won an international competition to design a huge office and retail complex. When completed in 2003, their building will be the first sky-scraper in Shanghai designed and built by a German firm.

Wan Xiang International Plaza is situated in the center of Shanghai at Nanjing Road, China's heavily populated shopping street, with more than two million customers passing through each day. Exposed to such heavy traffic, the development incorporates a ten-story retail center housing more than 150 shops, restaurants, and entertainment facilities. The center is expected to serve 250,000 visitors daily. A semi-transparent arcade functions as a linear connection between the building and the spacious, landscaped plaza on Nanjing Road, intended to attract pedestrians into the mall.

The most spectacular part of the develop-ment, however, is the fifty-two-story skyscraper adjacent to the retail center. Based on a triangular plan with a central, triangular service core, the tower reaches a height of 1,056 feet (325 meters), including its antenna. The double-skin, glass facade distinctively exposes the concrete-filled steel frame, in which diagonal struts not only emphasize the filigree-like design but also absorb forces arising from earthquakes. In contrast to many American-built sky-scrapers, the Chinese client requested an energy-efficient, naturally ventilated facade, based on German technology and experience with sustainable architecture—as Overdiek pointed out in an article in the *Rheinische Post* (December 12, 1996). Overdiek's firm became well known for their ecologically oriented, high-rise, RWE office building (1994–97) in Essen, Germany. Other special contextual requirements for the Shanghai project were a subway station in the lower level and parking facilities for 300 cars and more than 2,000 bicycles—the latter still the primary mode of wheeled transport in China.

Bird's-eye view of the model

Facade detail on the model

Model

Pudong, Shanghai

Numerous skyscrapers recently under construction or in planning in Shanghai exemplify the current economic expansion, helping make the city one of the most vivid examples of recent hyper-growth and developing consumerism in Asia. In 1990, to encourage international investment and entrepreneurship, the Chinese government declared Pudong—Shanghai's most prosperous district situated along the Huangpu River and located directly across from Old Town and the historical avenue, The Bund—as one of five coastal "Special Economic Zones" and free trade areas. With the advantages of rich resources, ecomomic privileges, and the city's favorable geographical location at the intersection of China's coast and waterways, international entrepreneurs are highly encouraged to invest in Shanghai's market. In contrast, strict regulations are imposed on foreign architectural firms working in China. Because private business is not permitted, foreign firms must be affiliated with a Chinese company, which is in charge of a building's execution.

Since skyscrapers always have been monuments of prosperity, wealth, and corporate capitalism, clients of Pudong's projects favor buildings as tall and as modern as possible. Though the projects presented here are not part of the fanatic contest for the world's tallest building, they are significant examples of skyscrapers shooting up in Shanghai's "forest of concrete."

Computer-generated view of the lobby

Shanghai Information Center

Architect	Nikken Sekkei Ltd., Tokyo, Japan
Structural Engineer	Nikken Sekkei Ltd.
Client	Shanghai Information World Co. Ltd.
Location	Pudong, Shanghai, People's Republic of China
Date	Estimated construction May 1997 – December 2002

Facing the 325-foot (100-meter) wide main road of the prospering business district, Nikken Sekkei's forty-three-story Shanghai Information Center represents another gateway tower in the Pudong Development Area. Designed as an integrated office complex consisting of a telecommunications and information museum, regional telecommunications equipment rooms, administrative offices, and tenant office spaces, the 926-foot (285-meter) tower, including its antenna, symbolizes the modernity of contemporary information industries in China.

The design of the facade emphasizes the building's different functions. Horizontal strips of continuous windows and aluminum spandrels indicate the location of the main

Computer-generated view
from street level

telecommunication facilities at the middle of the tower, while a half-mirror, glass curtain wall signals the location of the upper levels and their office floors. A two-story parapet screens the penthouses and utilities units on the roof. Its integrated fins, which function as air-intake louvers, and the exposed communication antenna emphasize the vertical elongation of the building's top. A rigid frame structure combined with a twin-core system allows for large, column-free office floors and a column-free atrium at the ground-floor level, the height of which is almost 109 feet (33.5 meters).

The enormous open space of the atrium is enclosed by a glass curtain wall that reveals inner elements of the building, including a sphere suspended from the seventh floor truss and a glass cube. Both are part of the telecommunications museum now open to the public.

Lujiazui-Itochu Building

Architect	Sydness Architects, P. C., New York, New York, USA
Associate Architect	Shanghai Institute of Architectural Design and Research
Structural Engineer	Leslie E. Robertson Associates
Client	Lujiazui-Itochu Development Co., Ltd.
Location	Pudong, Shanghai, People's Republic of China
Date	Estimated construction June 1998 – 2001

Another high rise in Pudong, the Lujiazui-Itochu Building by Sydness Architects, will not compete with its neighbors in terms of height, as it is only twenty-five stories high. However, the building maximizes ground-floor area in its floor plan, which is composed of two semi-circles that are shifted along the diameter. Its undulating curtain wall of polished granite is accented by vertical granite ribs that rise to a stepped roofline. This setback structure not only emphasizes the building's vertical extension, but adds a maximum amount of profitable corner offices. Additionally, the new corporate tower incorporates a large atrium rather than a retail podium on its ground floor. This is expressed on its facade by a horizontal arrangement of stone mullions, glass spandrels, and a recessed circular glazed entry.

Looking ahead in the twenty-first century, it is expected that as soon as the "sick Asian tiger" recovers, many similar projects now on hold will resume in Pudong. In scale and design it is likely that they will overtake Shanghai's historical district regardless of its traditional urban structure and architecture. So far, many three- and four-story residential buildings have been demolished, uprooting hundreds of thousands of people— all to make way for skyscrapers.

Site plan

Rendering of the project
in its urban context

China Insurance Building

Architect	The Webb Zerafa Menkes Housden Partnership (WZMH), Toronto, Canada
Associate Architect	East China Architectural Design and Research Institute
Structural Engineer	Quinn Dressel & Associates
Client	People's Insurance Company of China
Location	Pudong, Shanghai, People's Republic of China
Date	Completed 1999

Shanghai Pudong Development Bank

Architect	The Webb Zerafa Menkes Housden Partnership (WZMH), Toronto, Canada
Associate Architect	East China Architectural Design and Research Institute
Structural Engineer	Quinn Dressel Associates
Client	Shanghai Pudong Development Bank
Location	Pudong, Shanghai, People's Republic of China
Date	Estimated construction 1996 – July 2000

View of the lobby,
Shanghai Pudong Development Bank

The concept of mixed-use buildings having lower levels open to the public guided the design of WZMH's China Insurance Building and Shanghai Pudong Development Bank, both adjacent to the Shanghai Securities Exchange Building, completed by WZMH in 1997.

Located in the heart of Pudong, the Lujiazui finance and trade zone was developed especially for financial institutions and insurance companies; it has become the most important trading center in the Pacific Rim area.

Situated in this area of office towers, WZMH's thirty-eight-story insurance building includes a four-story retail and multi-use podium that is open to the public. Similarly, its thirty-four-story bank building is open to the public on the lower eight floors.

The insurance building culminates in circular twin beacons and slender mast structures that form a distinctive rooftop silhouette, especially at night. The Shanghai Pudong Development Bank conforms to the same tripartite division of podium, middle, and top. A huge, illuminated lantern crowned by a spire characterizes the tower's roof, while the base is dominated by a six-story arch that serves as an entrance. To enforce the notion of solidity in spite of a preponderance of exterior glass, the Bank's piers and spandrels are clad in stone and granite, instead of metal, as used on the office floors.

Rendering of the China Insurance Building

Model of the Shanghai Pudong Development Bank

21 Century Tower

Architect	Murphy/Jahn, Inc., Architects, Chicago, Illinois, USA
Associate Architect	East China Architectural Design & Research Institute
Structural Engineers	Maunsell Consultants Asia Ltd.
	Werner Sobek Engineers GmbH
Client	Shanghai 21 Century Center Real Estate Co. Ltd.
Location	Pudong, Shanghai, People's Republic of China
Date	Completion expected 2001

The building's location (1) on Pudong's east-west ceremonial axis

On April 18, 1990, the Chinese government announced plans to develop Shanghai's Pudong area in an effort to revitalize greater Shanghai as a center of international business and finance. Geographically, Pudong is ideal for such a plan since it is located at the mid-point of the Asian economic corridor that includes Seoul, Korea, and Tokyo, Japan, to the north and Hong Kong, Singapore, and Kuala Lumpur, Malaysia to the south. Moreover, Pudong is adjacent to the East China Sea in the east and the Yangtze River in the north, both of which provide an efficient mode of transportation necessary to support the demands of an international center.

One of the integral functional, as well as symbolic, requirements for any modern business and finance center is the skyscraper. Murphy/Jahn's 21 Century Tower is one of several skyscrapers in Pudong designed by Western architects. In an effort to contextualize the Pudong skyscrapers, one of the most popular Western design solutions is to appropriate Asian architectural forms such as the pagoda. While the 21 Century Tower's design clearly references Chinese architectural traditions by the liberal use of red on its structurally expressive elements, the design does not recreate historic Chinese architecture. Instead, the tower's geometrical, minimalist design—which is "high tech" not only aesthetically but mechanically— looks forward to a new China.

The 21 Century Tower consists of two elements: a forty-eight-story tower and a three-story podium building. The steel-and-glass tower is defined structurally by the use of the braced tube. This advanced structural system permits the elimination of a supporting column at the building's northwest corner, which is also where Pudong's principal open space is located. The drama of this glazed architectural space—which is supported by a system of horizontal steel plates, vertical cables, and horizontal steel spars—is further heightened by four nine-story sky gardens that provide relaxing areas for the building's tenants.

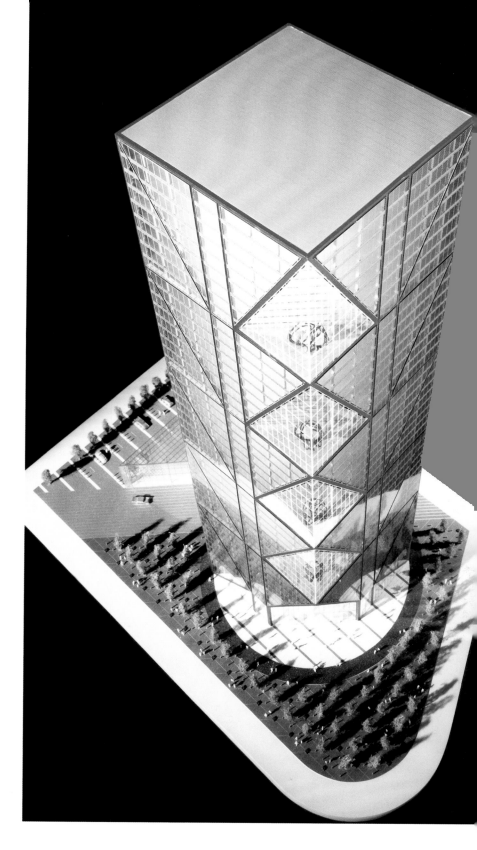

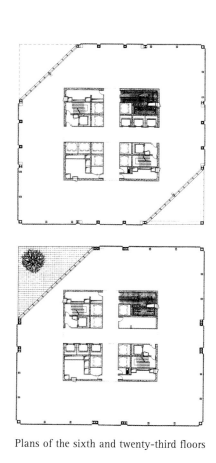

Plans of the sixth and twenty-third floors

Lobby detail: the illuminated
cylindrical glass core

Model

View of the tower
through the
atrium roof

Hotel tower

View of
the atrium

Jin Mao Tower

Architect	Skidmore, Owings & Merrill LLP, Chicago, Illinois, USA
Associate Architects	East China Architectural Design and Research Institute
Structural Engineer	Skidmore, Owings & Merrill LLP
Client	China Shanghai Foreign Trade Centre Company
Location	Pudong, Shanghai, People's Republic of China
Date	Completed 1999

In the first half of the 1990s, the Chinese economy expanded rapidly with an annual growth rate of thirteen percent. Positive economic projections—one of which forecast a seven-percent increase each year until the decade's end—resulted in a construction boom. Corresponding to the increase in construction was an increased demand for architects, which the Chinese market was unable to meet. Consequently, there were enormous opportunities for Western architects in China that were often not available in their own countries. One of the high-profile firms now designing Chinese skyscrapers is Skidmore, Owings & Merrill.

Located in the Pudong District of the Lujia-zui Finance and Trade Zone in Shanghai—Asia's financial center—the Jin Mao Tower is China's tallest. Approximately 1,380 feet (425 meters) tall, the eighty-eight-story skyscraper's extreme height required advanced structural engineering both to compensate for the area's unstable soil conditions and to enable the building to withstand the region's earthquakes and typhoons. Constructed of high-strength concrete and structural steel, the Jin Mao Tower's structure consists of an octagonal concrete core surrounded on four sides by

a pair of "supercolumns," which are large-scale, reinforced concrete supports. Three sets of eight two-story-high outrigger trusses connecting the columns to the core at six floors provide additional support to prevent the core's collapse.

If structural requirements impact the Jin Mao Tower's design, they do not determine it. Characteristic of many Western architects' approaches to Asian skyscraper design, Skidmore, Owings & Merrill's Adrian Smith attempted to contextualize the Jin Mao Tower by appropriating the language of Asian visual culture. The stepped-back form of the tower thus evokes the traditional forms of Chinese architecture, even while the tower's large-scale, modern materials and structure ground it in the present day.

View of
the tower

Sketch of the
pinnacle

Jakarta Stock Exchange at Sudirman Central Business District

Architect	Brennan Beer Gorman/Architects, New York, New York, USA
Associate Architect	JSEB Local Design Consortium
Structural Engineer	Beca Carter Hollings & Ferner, Ltd., New Zealand
Clients	P. T. Danaresksa Jakarta International
Location	Jakarta, Indonesia
Date	Completed 1997

View of the lobby

The Jakarta Stock Exchange Building

The Sudirman Central Business District (almost 100 acres or forty hectares) was planned by Philip Cox Richardson Taylor & Partners as a monumental and newly organized city core in order to "demonstrate to the world Jakarta's rising economic status and its cultural and political importance as well as to reinforce Jakarta's participation in South East Asian commerce, trade, and technology" (*Master Plan Report*).

In this business district's plan, office and residential towers, and retail facilities in lower and underground levels, are grouped around a huge landscaped open public space, all connected by pedestrian walkways, circular roads, vehicular tunnels, and underground parking. But due to the 1998 financial crisis in Asia, only the thirty-two-story Jakarta Stock Exchange has been completed. Construction on the forty-two-story Conrad International Hotel was stopped after it reached the seventh-floor framing, and plans for two towers for office and residential use, a three-story mall, and the thirty-four-story Financial Tower are indefinitely on hold.

BBG/A's design for the Stock Exchange consists of two office towers, connected by a common lobby, and a four-story podium which houses the trading room and support facilities. Each tower is composed of three equilateral triangles of varying heights, and the upper seven floors of each building are stepped back, visually reducing their overall mass.

The vertical movement of the towers is emphasized by light gray, polished granite piers that continue above the top floors, and contrast with darker gray, recessed granite spandrels and reflective silver glass on the facade. The interior lobby is decorated with highly polished marble and fountains lending the complex an affluent business environment. The Financial Tower has been designed to mirror the Stock Exchange Building in layout, massing, and materials, and although the construction documents were completed in 1994 that building is still awaiting the recovery of the Asian economy.

Partial view of model of the Sudirman Central Business District: Jakarta Stock Exchange Building, top left; Financial Tower, top right; and Conrad International Hotel, center

Atrium

Nadya Park

Architect	Kaplan McLaughlin Diaz, San Francisco, California, USA
Associate Architect	Daiken Sekkei
Structural Engineer	Daiken Sekkei
Client	City of Nagoya
Location	Nagoya, Japan
Date	Completed 1996

In 1991, the architectural firm of Kaplan McLaughlin Diaz (KMD) won an international competition, sponsored by the City of Nagoya, to design the new, one million-square-foot (90,000-square-meter) Nadya Park. This project marked the first development of the downtown area and an important announcement of Nagoya's emergence as Japan's design capital.

Nadya Park is composed of two distinctive glass-and-polished aluminum towers connected by a soaring, 165-foot (50-meter) atrium. The project combines public and private space within two distinguished towers. The fourteen-story Design Center houses a 300-seat, multi-purpose hall, a 700-seat theater, a design center with retail, display, and educational facilities, and a youth center. As KMD explains in its design statement: "the building itself is a celebration of abstract sculpture and modern design, integrating diverse geometric patterns into its profile, facade, and building features."

The adjacent twenty-three-story commercial tower features a seven-story retail podium with office floors above. Its convex tower, with floor-to-ceiling glazing, is topped by a giant, forty-foot (12.5-meter) metallic screen and elliptical crown which conceal the building's mechanical systems and helicopter pad.

Connecting both is a seven-story atrium flooded with natural light from a glass ceiling and front facade. Its exposed frames and ducts create a modern, high-tech atmosphere in which design elements from the two towers are subtly repeated. Contemporary works of art also hang in the atrium, although with its irregular balconies, open stairways, and glass elevators the atrium itself is a work of art. Since the completion of Nadya Park, the atrium has functioned as one of the city's most popular public venues—a forum for cultural activities in the heart of historic Nagoya.

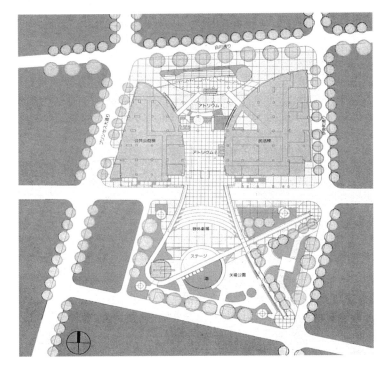

Site plan

The two-tower complex
with atrium

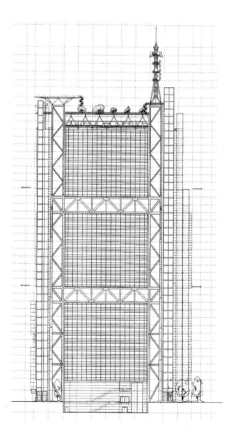

Concept design, 1997,
Nippon Television Headquarters (NTV)

Nippon Television Headquarters

Architect	The Richard Rogers Partnership, London, England
Structural Engineer	Ove Arup & Partners
	Mitsubishi Estate Co., Ltd.
Client	Nippon Television Headquarters
Location	Tokyo, Japan
Date	Design 1996, construction on hold

Seoul Broadcasting Centre

Architect	The Richard Rogers Partnership, London, England
Structural Engineer	Buro Happold
Client	Seoul Broadcasting System (SBS)
Location	Seoul, Korea
Date	Design 1996, construction on hold

World-renowned for his key buildings in Europe—including the Centre Pompidou in Paris, built with Renzo Piano (1971–77), and the Lloyd's Building in London (1978–86)—Richard Rogers is breaking new ground with different projects in Asia. In 1996, he won two separate international competitions for corporate communications headquarters in Japan and Korea. Both telecommunications towers incorporate various studios, production and programming areas, large numbers of office floors, and satellite dishes and broadcasting antennae. Both also conform to Rogers's characteristic use of exposed steel and concrete and his emphasis on distinguishing between structural and service components.

The Nippon tower in Tokyo will reach approximately 700 feet (215 meters) and will contain shops, restaurants, a public auditorium, and an art gallery. The first design of the tower referred to its function as a television headquarters: a huge square section of the facade was set back slightly to recall a television monitor. The revised design, however, emphasizes the steel-frame structure of the tower with exposed elevators on the outer skin of the facade.

The Seoul Broadcasting Centre in Korea was first planned as a twin tower complex, composed of forty-two levels above ground. Providing more than 1,076,400 square feet (100,000 square meters) of gross floor area, the two high rises were intended to be the tallest buildings in the developing high-rise district of Seoul. Ultimately, the project was modified to a single tower scheme, including a low-rise studio complex that is connected to the office tower by a spectacular thirteen-story atrium. Both the Tokyo and Korean towers have been postponed because of the financial crises in Southeast Asia in 1998.

South elevation of the
Seoul Broadcasting Centre tower

First design, NTV

Design model,
NTV

Model,
Seoul Broadcasting Centre

Menara UMNO

Architect	T. R. Hamzah & Yeang Sdn Bhd, Selangor, Malaysia
Structural Engineer	Tahir Wong Sdn Bhd
Client	South East Asia Development Corporation, Berhad
Location	Pulau Pinang, Malaysia
Date	Completed 1998

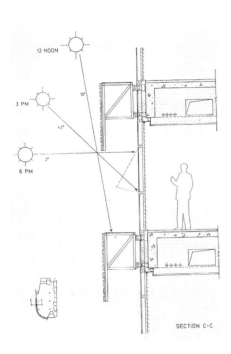

Diagram of the projective sunshades
and recessed ribbon windows

Technological innovation has historically been a significant impetus for the transformation of skyscraper design, as is the case in the late twentieth century, where new environmental technologies have had considerable impact on architecture. Malaysian architect Ken Yeang, author of *The Skyscraper Bioclimatically Considered*, is at the forefront of environmentally sensitive skyscraper design. His bioclimatic—also described as green or "sustainable"—approach to skyscraper design incorporates passive, low-energy technologies to minimize the environmental impact of a tall building. This approach also maximizes the comfort level of the building's occupants by allowing natural light and air into what have been traditionally hermetic environments. Each bioclimatic skyscraper is therefore site-

specific, since the natural environment of each location must be considered in order for the design to be effective.

In Malaysia, where the climate is humid and warm year-round, skyscrapers are typically air-conditioned. However, the twenty-one-story Menara UMNO ("menara" is the Malay term for tower, and UMNO is the acronym for the predominant political party in Malaysia) office building has windows that open, permitting natural ventilation when conditions are suitable, as well as air-conditioning. Moreover, employees' desks are located no more than twenty feet from an operable window in order to ensure that each worker has access to natural air and light. Extreme light is modified by sunshades that project from recessed tiers of ribbon windows.

Another bioclimatic feature is the building's specially designed wing-walls that direct wind to specific balcony zones. These "airlocks" provide comfortable, natural ventilation. Natural light and ventilation are also provided for the lobbies, staircases, and restrooms, thereby decreasing the building's overall energy consumption. The Menara UMNO's design, which addresses nature in terms of both site and sustainability, is the embodiment of Yeang's "holistic approach" to skyscraper design.

The building in
its urban context

View of the building's
sculptural qualities

Wind wing-wall

Telekom Malaysia

Architect	Hijjas Kasturi Associates, Kuala Lumpur, Malaysia
Structural Engineer	Ranhill Bersekutu
Client	Telekom Malaysia Berhad
Location	Kuala Lumpur, Malaysia
Date	Completion delayed indefinitely

A 1,007-foot (310-meter) tower now occupies a central position in the new Telekom Malaysia complex, flanked by a 1,500-seat auditorium and interactive exhibition and education center to the east and Telekom staff facilities including health, fitness, medical, and day-care centers to the west. Cafeterias and restaurants on two terraced levels face north towards the river.

The linear site determines the east-west elongation of the tower and reduces its eastern and western frontages—an ideal condition for a tropical structure as it minimizes the building's direct exposure to sunlight. To further reduce heat problems, large, open-air sky gardens have been incorporated into the tower's eastern and western sides. Alternating every third floor, and structurally supported by prefabricated steel trusses that protrude up to 107 feet (33 meters), these sky gardens help to reduce the visual impact of the height of the tower and provide all fifty-five occupied floors with access to landscaped, outdoor areas.

According to the architects, the shape of the tower was strongly influenced by the work of the Malaysian sculptor and painter Latiff Mahidin. Thus, it consists of two conical and convex slabs which appear to overlap and roll up on one side and unfold and open up on the other side, replicating "[a] new sprout shooting up from the earth, with solid roots to anchor it and the beauty of an unfurling leaf." The organic nature of the tower is an attempt to balance traditional regional forms and decoration with modern construction systems and high-tech equipment. A symbol of the fast-growing telecommunications market and of Telekom Malaysia as a provider of high technology, the building features advanced telecommunications systems and energy-efficient mechanical and electrical systems including individually controlled temperature, air, and light.

The building under construction

Opposite:
Model

Landscaped
outdoor terraces

Ground floor plan of Petronas Towers
and Kuala Lumpur City Centre

Petronas Towers

Architect	Cesar Pelli & Associates, New Haven, Connecticut, USA
Associate Architect	Adamson Associates
Structural Engineers	Thornton-Tomasetti Engineers
	Ranhill Bersekutu Sdn. Bhd.
Clients	Kuala Lumpur City Centre Holdings Sendirian, Berhad
	Kuala Lumpur City Centre, Berhad
Location	Kuala Lumpur, Malaysia
Date	Completed 1998

At 1,483 feet (452 meters) tall, the Petronas Towers in Kuala Lumpur, Malaysia constitute the world's tallest building. But as Blair Kamin's *Chicago Tribune* headline indicates—"Sears Tower Doesn't End Reign Without a Fight" (April 13, 1996)—the Petronas Towers' claim to the title was not without controversy, particularly regarding how a building's height should be measured. According to the Council on Tall Buildings and Urban Habitat—the organization that confers the "World's Tallest Building" title—a building's height extends to its structural top. This includes the Petronas Towers' spires but not the Sears Tower's broadcast antennas—since the former are considered to be integral to the building's design, while the latter are considered additions.

Ultimately, the question of whether the Petronas Towers are taller than the Sears Tower is less important than the economic and social conditions responsible for the large-scale shift of skyscraper construction from the U. S. cities of Chicago and New York to cities in Asia such as Kuala Lumpur and Shanghai. The proliferation of tall buildings in Asia reflects a similar set of economic conditions that, in large part, engendered skyscraper construction in late nineteenth-century American cities. These

include a rapidly expanding capitalist economy and escalating land values. However, it is important to recognize that Asian skyscrapers reflect not only the adoption of Western-style capitalism, but also a corresponding set of ideals, which the skyscraper embodies in architectural form. In effect, as Cesar Pelli, Charles Thornton, and Leonard Joseph wrote in *Scientific American*, the Petronas Towers "stand as a symbol of Malaysia's economic growth, while emphasizing the distinctly Islamic traditions of this southeast Asian nation. . . ." (December 1997).

And while the skyscraper has traditionally been associated with the United States, one of the most important considerations for Western architects designing Asian skyscrapers has been to have their buildings reflect their Asian context. For the Petronas Towers, Cesar Pelli's design was generated by a floor plan whose geometric circle-and-square design symbolized the principles of harmony in Islam. Thus, the Petronas Towers are contextual in design, if not in scale.

Facade detail

View of the building
in its urban context

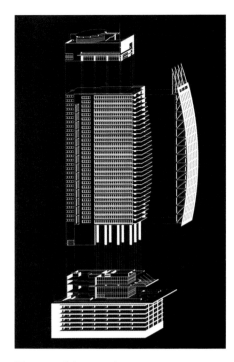

Diagram of the tower's component parts

Model

AMA Tower

Architect	Perkins & Will, Chicago, Illinois, USA
Associate Architect	Luis & Associates
Structural Engineer	Narciso S. Padilla Engineers
Clients	AMA Land
	Daewoo Corporation
Location	Metro Manila, Philippines
Date	Completion late 2000/early 2001

Perkins & Will's thirty-seven-story office building is located in Metro Manila's Mandaluyong area, one of its most rapidly developing sections. Recently praised by *Architecture*'s Ned Cramer for being on "the cutting edge of corporate architecture" (February 1998), the AMA Tower, designed by Ralph E. Johnson, has been imaginatively integrated into its commercial context through the distinctively nautical shape of its contoured, northern facade. This projects from the tower's otherwise rectangular massing, symbolically propelling the building like a ship along what Johnson describes as the "river of asphalt and concrete roadways." The ephemeral image of the tower floating away reflects the building's function as a temporary living and working space for foreign businessmen. As Johnson has recognized, "this analogy does gain power from the fact that the Philippines is a series of islands and has a long nautical history." The tower's vertical element can likewise be convincingly read as a metaphoric shield, protecting the building from its intrusive environment.

However, the function of the tower's massing is more than symbolic. Its tripartite organization also reflects functional differences. The base, which incorporates the first floor and two mezzanine levels, contains the building's public areas, including a lobby and retail stores. The extensive use of inviting floor-to-ceiling sections of glass in three of the building's four sides reflects its public function. In contrast to the open design of the base, the central section incorporating levels three to thirty-four is defined from the exterior by a grid of curtain wall. It contains offices and a hotel, while the tower's exclusive top levels accommodate what will either be penthouse apartments or offices.

Project rendering

Scotts Tower

Architect	Ong & Ong Architects Pte Ltd, Singapore
Structural Engineer	Steen Consultants Pte Ltd
Client	Far East Organization Pte Ltd
Location	Singapore
Date	Completion expected late 2001

Model

According to Ong & Ong, the Scotts Tower will set a standard for modern living in the twenty-first century. Their tower clearly differs from earlier housing projects in Singapore, where the island's weak economy, dense population, and increased demand for housing resulted in plain, rectangular tower blocks, interspersed with greenery, as the common residential form. Though their tower is situated in Singapore's most popular business district, Ong & Ong claim that they will not concede to the pressures of efficiency or financial concerns but will instead promote quality and aesthetics in design (*World Architecture*, July/August 1998).

At 299 feet (92 meters) high, excluding its antenna, the Scotts Tower contains two luxury apartments on each of its twenty-three floors. Although elliptical in appearance, the tower's interior layout conforms to conventional rectangular arrangements.

Its facade is defined by a number of interlocking elliptical bodies that recall the dynamic designs of early twentieth-century architects such as Erich Mendelsohn and members of the Bauhaus. Its overall elliptical form is disrupted by a rectangular wall on the southwest side. Also, the facade is recessed on the opposite side, marking the division of the two units on each floor. The lower half of the tower is defined by horizontal ribbon windows that are set in wide, protruding frames and wrap around the building's corner. Aluminum fins at the shifting of the ellipse function as visual extensions of these horizontal components.

On top of the tower, the mechanical plant is hidden behind elliptical louvers which are, in turn, crowned by a metal-clad, hyperbolic plane that is pierced by a mast. With its striking architectural forms and full-height, blue-tinted glass windows, the Scotts Tower vividly invokes the streamlined design favored by architects at the beginning of the twentieth century.

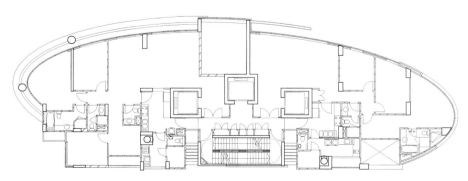

Typical floor plan

Baiyoke Tower II

Architect	Plan Architect Co., Ltd., Bangkok, Thailand
Structural Engineer	Arun Chaiseri Consulting Engineers Co., Ltd.
Client	Land Development Co., Ltd.
Location	Bangkok, Thailand
Date	Completed 1999

Rendering of the tower in its urban context

Both Baiyoke Tower I, completed in 1987, and Tower II, completed in 1999, are situated in one of the most dense and congested districts of Bangkok. Sited in an old warehouse district, the two towers rise above mostly small-scale, older neighbors.

At 1,050 feet (320 meters) high, Baiyoke Tower II was designed to be the tallest building in Asia. However, it has already been surpassed by the Petronas Towers in Kuala Lumpur (see pp. 82-83). In an attempt to regain the title, owner Panlert Baiyoke, Chairman of Land Development, is now planning to put a communication tower and antenna on the building's roof. With these additions, the tower will be 1,495 feet (460 meters) high and again a contender in the ongoing race for the world's tallest building.

In Thailand, as in Southeast Asia, labor is cheaper than high technology. Consequently, the tower was erected via a high-strength, cast-in-place concrete method, making the ninety-story tower the world's highest reinforced concrete structure. It rises out of a massive, red-hued concrete base like "the image of natural sandstone rising from the earth." The facade of its upper levels repeatedly steps back until it reaches the circular top where the glittering gold color, a traditional Thai element symbolizing wealth, defines its silhouette and emphasizes the building's vertical extension.

The tower, with its nineteen floors of shops, restaurants, car parks, and service areas is mainly used by the luxury Baiyoke Sky Hotel. With an estimated daily use of 112,608 kW of electricity and 792,600 gallons (3,000 cubic meters) of water, the tower's consumption exceeds that of some small provinces in Thailand. This has forced the Bangkok Metropolitan Administration to request the construction of a proper sewage system.

Detail of
the tower base

The tower
nearing
completion

SEG Apartment Tower

Architect	Coop Himmelb(l)au, Vienna, Austria
Structural Engineer	Projektierungsbüro für Industrie-, Hoch- und Tiefbauten AG
Client	SEG Stadterneuerungs- und Eigentums-wohnungsgesellschaft m. b. H.
Location	Vienna, Austria
Date	Completed 1998

Facade detail

Established by Viennese architects Wolf D. Prix and Helmut Swiczinsky in 1968, Coop Himmelb(l)au produces avant-garde work by means of the group's engagement in political, social, and theoretical discourse. Corresponding to Michel Foucault's idea that "every form is actually a compound of forces," Coop Himmelb(l)au draw inspiration from the ever-changing form of the cloud. The cloud, the architects observe, "is a differential system rather than an object. It alludes identity by being a product of the complex web of influences in which it finds itself, rather than of specific intention. In this way, the cloud as method threatens to erode the control of the architectural designer, thereby opening up new fields of spatial possibility."

The disjunctive exterior form of Coop Himmelb(l)au's twenty-five-floor SEG Apartment Tower suggests that the building is a "compound of forces." Conceived as the superimposition of two buildings, the tower contains seventy apartments and nine commercial units. The area between the two differentiated sections functions as the main social space and houses a multi-purpose room, a children's playroom, a "teleworking café," and a sun deck. The tower's dramatic design not only expresses the architects' interest in dynamic, flexible forms, but its glass "climate" facade and roof "air box" also serve to cool the apartments in the summer and heat them in the winter.

Opposite:
View from street level

Interior view

Swiss Re London Headquarters

Architect   Foster and Partners, London, England
Structural Engineer   Ove Arup & Partners
Client   Swiss Reinsurance Company
Location   London, England
Date   Design 1998

View at night

Opposite:
Photomontage showing urban context

Located in the heart of London's financial district, this building will house the headquarters of the largest life and health reinsurer in the world, Swiss Reinsurance. In an attempt to develop a humane space within an urban context, the building's architects, Foster and Partners, have been sensitive to the surrounding landscape. Their concern for natural light and air and inviting social spaces for tenants and the general public is evident in the building's design. Diagonally braced and wrapped in glazing, the structure will rise 590 feet (180 meters) from its island site and have a new public space at its base. At forty-one stories, plus a basement, it will contain 450,000 square feet (137,160 square meters) of floor space. The main lobby will lead into a double-height arcade housing two levels of retail space.

By rotating each successive floor, Foster and Partners have created voids at the edges of each floor plate which will form a series of spiral atria. To assist in ventilation, they have incorporated horizontal slots into the atria which will draw in natural air at each floor. Additionally, they will have enclosed the atria at every sixth floor to allow for gardens and social spaces for the tenants. Upon completion, the ground floor will open up the base of the building via low stone walls, trees, and retail kiosks, making the area into what the architects call a "new point of destination" and a "fluid public domain." Outside of the main tower, a six-story, glass-and-stone building will be constructed to house a new café, its management offices, and plant. The entire complex will occupy a site bounded by Bury Street, Bury Court, Browns Buildings, and St. Mary Axe in London.

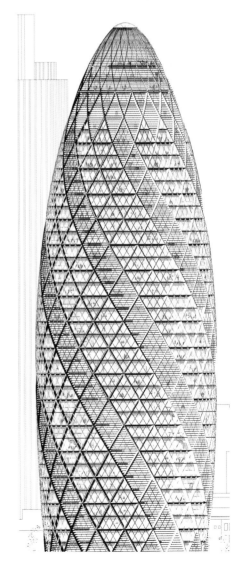

East elevation, Bury Street

Rendering of the lobby

Hongkong and Shanghai Banking Corporation London Headquarters

Architect	Foster and Partners, London, England
Structural Engineer	Ove Arup & Partners
Client	Canary Wharf Contractors (DS2) Limited; HSBC
Location	London, England
Date	Estimated construction January 1999 – 2001

With curved corners and a surface of sheer glass, HSBC's "transparent" tower will stand 656 feet (200 meters) high in London's Canary Wharf district, and be topped by an illuminated halo. Designed around a central core with open-plan floors, the building will provide 1.1 million square feet (335,280 square meters) of interior space for the bank's main facilities. The tower, deemed "economical and state of the art" by those involved in its construction, will be HSBC's first building to house all 800 of its departments within one structure.

The main lobby will be 92 feet (28 meters) in height and will lead via escalator to three 19-foot high trading halls. Thirty-nine floors will be utilized as office space, with three floors provided for transferring passengers between elevator groups. Below ground, three levels of parking and a direct link to the London Underground will be available. The tower's architects, Foster and Partners, are already known for their internationally acclaimed Hongkong and Shanghai Banking Corporation Hong Kong Headquarters (1985), widely recognized as a landmark.

Rendered exterior view

View of the main entry

25 Canada Square

Architect	Cesar Pelli & Associates, New Haven, Connecticut, USA
Structural Engineer	M. S. Yolles Partnership Limited, Toronto
Client	Canary Wharf Contractors (DS2) Limited
Location	London, England
Date	Estimated construction 1999 – 2001

This forty-two-story tower, some 650 feet (198 meters) high, will adjoin a seventeen-story building designed by Foster and Partners, presently under construction for Citibank. The two buildings will make up a Citigroup complex of 1.16 million square feet (353,568 square meters) designed to house 6,000 employees and to accommodate future expansion. The tower will step back at its top, and its overall massing will be similar to other Pelli-designed skyscrapers such as Battery Park City in New York City (1981) and 181 West Madison in Chicago (1990). For the London Citigroup tower, Pelli has designed a stainless-steel grid that will complement a similar, modular grid on the adjacent Citibank building by Foster and Partners.

Twenty-five Canada Square will be Pelli's second tower in Canary Wharf, the other being the fifty-story One Canada Square, completed in 1991 and considered one of England's first true skyscrapers. At 775 feet (236 meters) and forty-eight stories tall, this square prism culminates in a pyramid and includes not only offices and retail space, but also a light rail system that accommodates approximately 60,000 commuters daily.

Rendering of Citigroup complex; facade detail (bottom right)

Tour Hines

Architect	Pei Cobb Freed & Partners Architects LLP, New York, New York, USA
Associate Architect	Roger Saubot-Jean Rouit & Associates
Structural Engineer	SETEC TPI
Client	The Hines Corporation
Location	Paris, France
Date	Estimated construction 2000 – 2001/2002

In 1958, the French government began to develop La Défense, a business district meant to encourage economic activity. The first buildings constructed there were monolithic office towers which were criticized for being insensitively designed. By contrast, the design of the forty-one-story Tour Hines at La Défense was largely guided by Pei Cobb Freed & Partners' desire to be sensitive to the building's historically significant site: the last remaining parcel of land located along the elevated pedestrian mall of La Défense. Aligned with the Garden of La Défense on which it fronts, the Tour Hines continues the famous Louvre/Champs Elysées axis that terminates to the west in the Arc de Triomphe.

The Tour Hines' oval plan is reflected in the tower's curved glass walls. Also, a metal-and-glass canopy extends from the building's entrance, creating a sheltered place for visitors to congregate. Responsive features such as these reveal Pei Cobb Freed & Partners' conviction that their building be engaged with the extant Paris de la Défense and help enrich the public environment of La Défense.

Contrary to the mixed-use layout of most recent skyscrapers, the Tour Hines is primarily an office tower whose major tenant will occupy at least sixty percent of its square footage. Indeed, forty of the building's forty-one floors are dedicated to office space—the forty-first floor is reserved for mechanical functions and is therefore unoccupied.

Rendering by Paul Stevenson Oles
showing the overall massing

Ground floor plan

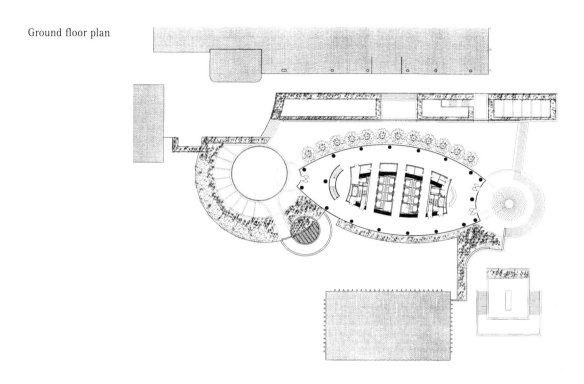

Detail of model showing the entry plaza

Detail of
the base

Computer-generated image
of the final design

Cœur Défense

Architect	Jean-Paul Viguier/s. a. d'architecture, Paris, France
Structural Engineer	Setec
Client	Unibail Paris/Tangra/Arc 108
Location	Paris, France
Date	Estimated construction 1998 – late 2000

Located at the very center of Paris's La Défense, Jean-Paul Viguier's Cœur Défense occupies one of the last available sites along the central Grand Axis that cuts through this commercial and residential district that has been developing since the late 1950s. Terminating this central axis is von Spreckelsen and Andreu's Grande Arche from 1989—one of President Mitterrand's "Grands Projets"— a symbolic landmark among the increasing number of skyscrapers in this district. The Cœur Défense forms a counterpoint to the Grande Arche and directs attention to its architectural importance.

The Cœur Défense soon will be the largest real estate development in this area, providing a gross floor area of over 3,767,400 square feet (350,000 square meters), 2,045,160 square feet (190,000 square meters) of which have been appropriated for office use. Viguier's first design consisted of a group of rectangular towers of differing heights, facing each other at right angles around a central square. However, his final design lacks these sharp corners and emphasizes the horizontal over the vertical. "A tower and its double" is Viguier's concept for the complex, which will consist of two identical thirty-eight-story towers and three similar, but lower, eight-story buildings—all perpendicular to the Grand Axis. All five buildings will have the same oblong floor plan and rounded design, although the two identical towers will be staggered in order to narrow and focus the view onto the Grande

Arche. A large 390 x 195 foot (120 x 60 meter) wide atrium connects the five high rises that Viguier describes as a "real microcosm" of a city, housing restaurants, gardens, fountains, shops, and elevators and circulation routes linking various spaces, including a conference center and museum of contemporary art. Instead of using tinted or reflective glazing, the entire complex is encased in a double skin of clear glass. This lack of surface treatment adds to the notion of transparency and lightness and is intended to attract the public into the complex.

Model of the first design

Tower detail

Opposite:
Model

Project in its urban context, with the
1972 Olympic complex in the foreground

High Rise at Olympia Park

Architect	Ingenhoven Overdiek und Partner, Düsseldorf, Germany
Structural Engineers	Leonhardt, Andra und Partner
	Boll und Partner
Client	REMU Grundstücksverwaltungsgesellschaft mbH
Location	Munich, Germany
Date	Estimated construction February 2000 – April 2003

While everyone thinks immediately of Frankfurt, the so-called Manhattan on the Main, or of Berlin's high-rise projects at Potsdamer Platz (pp. 101-103) upon seeing the word "skyscraper" paired with Germany, in Munich plans are underway to build Europe's tallest building: the Garden Tower in the new business park adjacent to the grounds of the 1972 Olympics.

Ingenhoven Overdiek und Partner won second prize in the international design competition for the tower in 1993. But after construction was postponed due to Germany's financial recession and oversupply of office space in Munich, the runners-up were commissioned to revise their scheme

in 1997. While a maximum height of 325 feet (100 meters) was stipulated in the original competition, the local Department of Building Instructions approved a 474-foot (146-meter) tower in August 1998. On the one hand, financial investment and efficiency were reasons for this extension. On the other, architect Ingenhoven insisted, in an interview in the *Süddeutsche Zeitung* (June 8, 1998), that according to his design theory, which is based, supposedly, on the antique understanding of ideal proportions, the tower, with its square plan of 117 x 117 feet (36 x 36 meters), needed to rise approximately 700 feet (216 meters) to fulfill the harmonious proportion of 1:6.

The tower will be divided into three individual units, each consisting of stacked floors suspended from certain other floors for structural transition. The developer proudly envisions the "ultimate skyscraper" with additional units that may be stacked to over 854 feet (263 meters), a height which would bestow the title of Europe's tallest skyscraper on the tower. However, building to this height would require the reconstruction of the central service core that stiffens the structure and carries the entire load of the tower. Similar to the firm's design of the Wan Xiang International Plaza in Shanghai (pp. 60-61), their use of transparent, floor-to-ceiling glazing on the facade will expose the construction underneath.

ARAG 2000 Tower

Architects	Rhode Kellermann Wawrowsky (RKW), Düsseldorf, Germany
	Foster and Partners, London, England
Structural Engineer	SPI Schüßler Plan
Client	Allgemeine Rechtsschutzversicherungs AG
Location	Düsseldorf, Germany
Date	Estimated construction November 1998 – February 2001

Model

"Towers in the Park" was the title of the 1990 concept for the new administration headquarters of the insurance company ARAG in northern Düsseldorf. In a joint venture with London-based Foster and Partners, RKW designed twin towers connected by a central glazed atrium. However, in 1995 the project was put on hold for two years in response to the recession that followed German reunification and as a result of the corporate reorganization of ARAG. Construction finally began in 1998—with a radically altered design—after the traffic system was reorganized and 1,625 feet (500 meters) of train track running through the site was moved.

The original twin-tower project was reduced to only one tower, decreasing the gross floor area from 602,784 square feet (56,000 square meters) to 344,448 square feet (32,000 square meters). The remaining 421-foot (129.5-meter) tower was also redesigned along an axially symmetrical plan. Flexible office units are now organized around an elliptical, inner atrium with open stairwells, while elevators, emergency stairs, and restrooms are located at each end of the plan. A double-glass, active ventilating facade reveals the interior concept: thirty floors divided into six-floor units separated by decentralized floors with enclosed garden terraces.

Adhering to Germany's interest in developing green high rises, a major effort has been made to protect the environment using energy-efficient technology. An innovative rear-ventilated facade produces a thermal stack effect and allows a natural exchange of fresh air, minimizing the need for conventional air-conditioning. Fresh air enters the offices through ventilation slots in the outer skin at floor level: the return air is expelled into the double facade underneath the ceiling. At every sixth floor the air is released via the louvered facade of the garden terrace. Likewise, the construction materials are consistent with Germany's policy of using natural resources. For instance, the glass facades that admit daylight into the building's interior can be controlled individually by natural oak shutters.

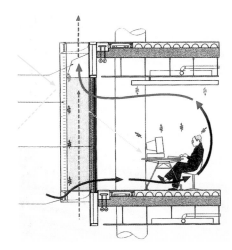

Diagram showing natural ventilation; the top left arrow represents direct sunlight

Model

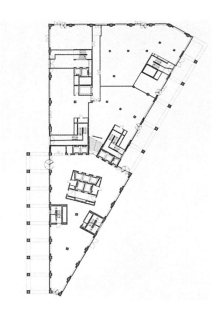

Ground floor plan

DaimlerChrysler Office Building

Architect	Architekten Kollhoff & Timmermann, Berlin, Germany
Associate Architect	Jaspar Jochimsen
Structural Engineer	Boll/Arup
Client	DaimlerChrysler AG
Location	Berlin, Germany
Date	Completed 1999

An enormous, mixed-use complex is currently being developed at Potsdamer Platz in the center of Berlin; this area has been a no-man's-land since the Berlin Wall was built across it in 1961. A new master plan by Hilmer and Sattler respects the district's historic block structure and street plan by recreating the main features of Leipziger and Potsdamer Platz in terms of their location and function. Once complete, three skyscrapers—by Kollhoff & Timmermann, Renzo Piano, and Helmut Jahn (pp. 102-103)—will form a tower block surrounding Potsdamer Platz that functions as an entry into this reinvented district. While the historical importance of the site and the outline of its former buildings are respected, the new skyscrapers lend a contemporary look to the city's skyline.

The DaimlerChrysler office and retail tower, developed by Hans Kollhoff, in association with Jaspar Jochimsen, is a reinforced-concrete structure with a base clad in red-brown brick and gray-green granite. It stands in sharp contrast to Piano's Debis Towers, clad in glass and terra-cotta, and to Helmut Jahn's glassy Sony Center.

One of the many regulations established during the construction boom following German reunification in 1990 stipulated that the building heights, materials, and forms of traditional buildings be "critically reconstructed" in new projects in Berlin. However, Kollhoff's triangular skyscraper was exempted from these height requirements. Its design follows the traditional set-back form of New York City skyscrapers, its upper levels moving back from the street and culminating in a twenty-two-story tower facing Potsdamer Platz. On the opposite side of the building, there is a glass-roofed atrium cut into the triangular floor plan, providing internal access to the tower and its two wings.

Both the Debis Towers and the Sony Center are controversial because their heights violate city regulations. Additionally, they have been accused of violating the urban character and public function of this new center of Berlin. Most of the buildings at the Potsdamer Platz complex are office buildings; thus, only their lower levels are open to the public. However, in conjunction with the adjacent mixed-use buildings, which include hotels, retail areas, theaters, cinemas, restaurants, and bars, the Potsdamer Platz development is intended to be a new type of urban area. Planners expect that more than ten thousand people will live and work in the complex. They also foresee hundreds of thousands of visitors daily.

Opposite:
Model of
the complex

Sony Center Berlin

Architect	Murphy/Jahn, Inc., Architects, Chicago, Illinois, USA
Structural Engineers	Ove Arup & Partners
	BGS
	Werner Sobek Engineers GmbH
Client	Sony Corporation
Location	Berlin, Germany
Date	Completion expected 2000

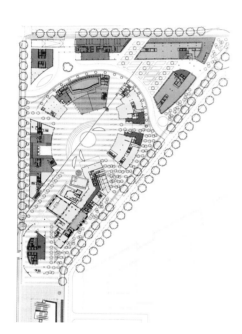

Site plan

Rendering of the Sony Forum

During the cornerstone laying ceremony speech for the Sony Center Berlin on October 11, 1996, the Chairman and CEO of Sony Corporation asserted that "With the epochal change in Europe . . . Berlin will not only be at the center of this new Europe geographically, but will also [. . .] become the economic and cultural center of the continent." This large-scale complex indicates the magnitude of the company's conviction.

Located in Berlin's historic Potsdamer Platz, the Sony Center's organization was determined by a pre-existing urban block structure established by Hilmer and Sattler in 1991. In response to what Murphy/Jahn criticized as the master plan's "static order and rigidity," the buildings are arranged so that spatial relationships are as interesting as the architectonic ones. The Sony Center incorporates three principal parts: the Hochhaus Potsdamer Platz, the Sony Headquarters, and the Sony Forum. The pedestrian experience is enlivened inside the block by a series of open, covered, and closed areas that accommodate pedestrian traffic and provide areas for repose. The Sony Center's organization also reflects a desire to relate the building's forms to adjacent areas such as Potsdamer Strasse, Kemper Platz, and Bellevue Park. Moreover, the building's design incorporates the extant remains of the famed Grand Hotel Esplanade, a luxury hotel from the early twentieth century that once hosted Kaiser Wilhelm II as well as film stars Charlie Chaplin and Greta Garbo. To accommodate the Esplanade, architect Helmut Jahn designed a structure containing modern housing that forms a bridge to the Esplanade, thereby creating an interesting juxtaposition between old and new.

The twenty-six-story Sony Center is an interesting variation on the multi-use skyscraper. While a prototypical skyscraper's multi-use functions are arranged vertically, with retail areas in the lower levels, business offices in the middle levels, and residential areas in the upper levels, the Sony Center's multi-use areas extend horizontally. Consequently, the Sony Headquarters is contained in a curved-glass tower, the Filmhaus and IMAX facilities are contained in the Sony Forum, and Sony's main office address is at the Hochhaus Potsdamer Platz.

Frankfurt

Frankfurt's increasing political, financial, and commercial importance as an international financial and service center—for example, it is home to the European Central Bank—finds architectural expression in the new urban development study entitled "Frankfurt 2000." The local firm Jourdan & Müller projects three high-rise clusters in downtown "Mainhattan"; the extension of the traditional banking quarter; a convention center; and a new, planned park quarter built over the train tracks leading to the main station. The development study includes fifteen new skyscrapers—among them a millennium tower that is intended to shoot up more than 1,186 feet (365 meters), stripping Norman Foster's Commerzbank (pp. 110-111) of the title of Europe's tallest building. Prior to this ambitious development and altitude boom, other towers were already under construction, with still others planned but waiting for investors and city building permits.

Romantic Tower

Architect	Architekten Kollhoff & Timmermann, Berlin, Germany
Structural Engineer	Ingenieurbüro Müller Marls GmbH
Client	Aachener und Münchener Lebensversicherung AG
Location	Frankfurt/Main, Germany
Date	Estimated construction Spring 1999 – Summer 2000

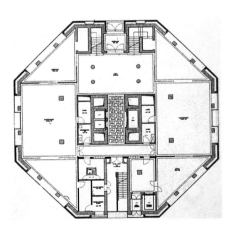

Typical high-rise floor plan

The American model of living in skyscrapers seems to have become a fashionable new trend in "Mainhattan." Developer Jocks Bock of the Deutschherrnviertel, a large development on the southern side of the Main River in the former slaughterhouse area, claims that his residential Romantic Tower is the first real New York skyscraper in Germany—although Hans Kollhoff's design of the twenty-three-story, brick-faced tower with bay windows recalls some of the European entries for the Chicago Tribune Tower competition in 1922. The overall design is defined by Kollhoff's characteristic, rigid grid of windows and a facade that steps back at the upper levels, like a Gothic tower cap. Golden, glazed tiles appear like Gothic pinnacles along the alternating rooflines, intensifying the vertical elongation of the building and its neo-gothic appearance. They are intended to compensate for the squat proportions of the tower, as its height is restricted to 293 feet (90 meters), according to a former master plan that restricted the construction of more high rises on the southern side of Frankfurt.

The developer requested an octagonal floor plan for the five-story podium. For this reason, Kollhoff grouped the apartments around a central service core which provides living rooms with panoramic views. In imitation of the American "doorman system," the tower's ground floor houses offices and service and dining facilities.

Computer-generated view
of the 'Romantic Tower'

Main Tower

Architect	Architekten Schweger + Partner, Hamburg, Germany
Structural Engineer	ARGE MAIN TOWER
Client	HELICON Verwaltungsgesellschaft mbH & Co Immobilien OHG
Location	Frankfurt/Main, Germany
Date	Completed 1999

Two neighboring towers rise in the center of Frankfurt's dense financial district, where building height symbolizes the corporate identity of innumerable banks, investment firms, and insurance companies: the 648-foot (199.5-meter) Main Tower, designed by Schweger + Partner, and the 331.5-foot (102-meter) Eurotheum by Novotny Mähner + Assoziierte.

The fifty-five-story Main Tower was designed as two geometric forms that are distinguished by their materials: a light and transparent glass cylinder and a slender, bronze-clad, square tower. Both sections are split into five below-grade parking levels, five podium levels, including the entrance lobby, a conference area, employee dining facilities, and fifty floors for office use. The top floors are occupied by restaurants and observation decks making Main Tower the first skyscraper in Frankfurt fully accessible to the general public. The top decks are reached by express elevators, which hold the German record for climbing up to twenty-three feet (seven meters) per second. The five-story podium of the tower is sheathed with the facade of the landmark building that formerly stood on the site—a building which was dismantled, stored, and reassembled upon completion of construction.

View of the
bronze-clad square tower

Far left, view of
the 'glass cylinder'

Rendering showing the curved glass elevator shaft

Eurotheum

Architect	Novotny Mähner + Assoziierte, Offenbach, Germany
Structural Engineer	Grebner Gesamtbauplanung GmbH
Client	COMMERZ GRUNDBESITZ Investmentgesellschaft mbH
Location	Frankfurt/Main, Germany
Date	Completed 1999

For the Eurotheum, Novotny Mähner + Assoziierte has completely removed the interior core of a six-story landmark building, while preserving its exterior—a method of construction also seen in Main Tower by Schweger + Partner. The original facade will encase a new low-rise structure that is connected to a thirty-one-story tower by a large glass atrium.

According to developer Köllmann AG, the Eurotheum will be the first modern skyscraper in Germany in which residential and office uses are combined. The twenty-one lower office floors and seven top floors of luxury apartments will be distinguished by different types of external cladding. In one corner, a curved service core with six elevators will be cut into the rectangular floor plan, and its curved, glass-clad elevator shaft will continue, uninterrupted, through all floors. The twenty-second floor, called the Eurolounge, will serve as an entrance and service area for the above residential floors. As in American doorman buildings, there will be special services available to Eurotheum residents, including laundry collection, reception, and security.

Interior view

View of
the tower

Commerzbank Headquarters

Architect	Foster and Partners, London, England
Structural Engineer	Ove Arup & Partners
Client	Commerzbank
Location	Frankfurt/Main, Germany
Date	Completed 1997

View from street level

Rising sixty stories or 849.73 feet (261.45 meters), Foster and Partners' Commerzbank Headquarters in Frankfurt is the tallest building in Europe. However, unlike Americans in cities such as Chicago and New York, which have historically competed to have the tallest skyscraper, the Germans are more ambivalent towards the Commerzbank's height. This ambivalence is reflected in the Commerzbank's energy-conserving design, which attempts to minimize the impact of the tower on the environment by integrating it into the existing scale of Frankfurt's financial center, while also providing a comfortable and flexible work environment.

In effect, as Peter Buchanan wrote in *Architecture + Urbanism*, popular and political demands for a green building essentially required Foster and Partners to "reinvent the skyscraper." In contrast to the hermetic environments of most modern skyscrapers, the design of the Commerzbank "turn[s] the conventional skyscraper inside-out, opening it up" (February 1998).

Energy consumption is thereby reduced by innovative double-glazed windows that are motorized, enabling the circulation of outside air when the offices are warm. Moreover, the triangular plan allows space for a central forty-nine-story, ventilating atrium by displacing service core elements—such as the structural columns, elevators, and utilities—to the tower's three corners. Such a configuration also allows each of the build-

ing's offices to benefit from an optimal amount of sunlight.

The inclusion of nine thematically planned gardens, each four stories high, also helps minimize the differences between indoor and outdoor environments—differences which were routinely reinforced in traditional skyscraper designs. The gardens also function as organizing elements within a tower conceived as a series of villages. Consequently, each garden acts as a village green. The village concept encourages a sense of community, which is reinforced by extensive interior glazing that reveals, rather than conceals, the workers and their activities.

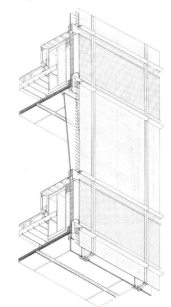

Isometric drawing
of the double-facade
tower cladding

Opposite:
View from across
the River Main

Generale Bank Tower

Architect	Murphy/Jahn, Inc., Architects, Chicago, Illinois, USA
Associate Architect	Inbo Architectenburo
Structural Engineer	3BN
Client	Generale Bank
Location	Rotterdam, The Netherlands
Date	Completed 1997

Detail of the entryway

In a *Wall Street Journal* article on contemporary Chicago architectural firms, Alexia Vargas wrote that "The city's most famous architects—Helmut Jahn, Adrian Smith and Dirk Lohan—are focused mainly overseas. . . ." (July 8, 1998). American architectural firms found building opportunities unavailable in the United States during the recession of the early 1990s. For example, Murphy/Jahn Architects opened two offices in Germany— one in Frankfurt and another in Munich—in response to their increasing number of European Commissions. The Generale Bank Tower in Rotterdam is one example of Murphy/ Jahn's intensified European presence.

Although the term "skyscraper" does not come immediately to mind when discussing The Netherlands, the country's second largest city, Rotterdam, has been described as "Manhattan on the Maas." Indeed, the tallest office building in The Netherlands, the Nationale Nederlanded Building, is in Rotterdam. Rotterdam has been able to accommodate modern commercial development easily because its city center was obliterated by German and Allied bombing during World War II. Among the few buildings spared were the city hall, the main post office, and the stock exchange. Rotterdam's new city center is an experiment in comprehensive city planning, with an awareness of site expressed by its sensitive orientation toward the river.

Murphy/Jahn's Generale Bank Tower is integrated into its urban context via a pedestrian-level square which provides spatial and visual continuity with the established environment and serves as a threshold to both Schielandshuis and Hoogstraat streets. The tower also responds to pre-existing site conditions: its wedge-like shape accommodates the daylight requirements of an adjacent apartment building, and its elevation creates a visual connection with the Maritime Museum. Likewise, the tower's curved facade responds to the canal, providing harbor views for its occupants.

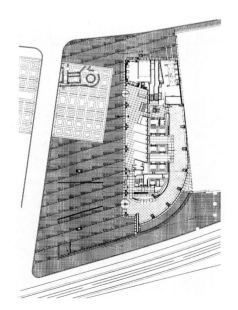

Site plan

View of
the tower

Warsaw Daewoo Center

Architect	RTKL Associates Inc., Baltimore, Maryland, USA
Associate Architect	MWH Architekci, Poland
Structural Engineer	RTKL International Ltd.
Client	Daewoo Corporation
Location	Warsaw, Poland
Date	Completed 1999

Following Japanese colonial rule of South Korea in the 1920s and 1930s, the South Korean government implemented a Japanese-influenced economic system to expand the country's position within the global market. The South Korean economy is organized as a series of *chaebol*, which are privately-owned companies with diversified holdings. While the *chaebol* are privately owned, they are nevertheless strictly controlled by governmental policies. In effect, the government determines the country's economic direction, described as "guided capitalism," which the *chaebol* then execute. In the late 1980s, the government promoted international expansion in industrial development. Daewoo Corporation, the third-largest South Korean *chaebol*, responded by entering into tarpaulin production in Vietnam and automobile production in Poland.

Daewoo is a conglomerate of twenty-four companies with interests that include construction, consumer electronics, financial services, telecommunications, and textiles. The name Daewoo translates as "Great Universe," a concept that is embodied in the company's logo, which Daewoo describes as a symbol "of the determination and development of Daewoo as it broadens to a wider world." Daewoo's future plans concentrate on global expansion in the automobile industry, as presented in company founder Kim Woo Chong's Vision 2000 strategy. A journalist for the *The Economist* noted that Daewoo's strategy "suggested that it had suddenly decided that Eastern Europe was a more promising market in the short run than emerging markets in Asia" (September 14, 1996).

RTKL's Warsaw Daewoo Center skyscraper is an emphatic expression of the company's confidence in Poland's economic potential. The forty-story company tower is a multi-use complex that includes office and retail spaces, restaurants, and a health club. Required to be economic in design and materials, the Center is composed of simple juxtapositions of curved and rectangular forms that progress from its semicircular atrium to its rectangular center to the reverse curve of its top. One of the tower's most dramatic elements is its entrance, which opens onto a five-story atrium that doubles as a winter garden and a display area for the client's latest lines of automobiles and electronics products.

Site plan

Opposite:
Model

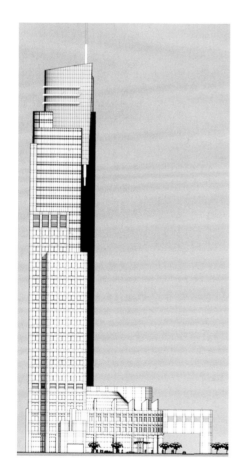

Elevation

Rendering of the marina complex

Model: the view from Beirut

Nara Towers

Architect	Perkins & Will, Chicago, Illinois, USA
Associate Architect	Dar Al-Handasah (Shair & Partners)
Structural Engineer	Dar Al-Handasah (Shair & Partners)
Client	HARDCO
Location	Beirut, Lebanon
Date	Completion expected 2001

Computer-generated sketches of waterfront views

Throughout history, tall buildings—as functionally, structurally, and stylistically dissimilar as the pyramids of Mykerinos, Cheops, and Chefren in Giza (c. 2570–2500 B. C.), the Eiffel Tower in Paris (1887–89) and Chicago's Sears Tower (1968–74)—have served as spectacular symbols of social aspirations. Like these structures, Nara Towers also represents community ideals. Following years of internal conflict, Beirut is again becoming a vibrant civic center connecting Europe with the Middle East. Nara Towers is an important aspect of this renewed development. The towers' distinct materials—one is constructed of glass and the other of stone—refer to the site, symbolizing Beirut as a city between mountain and sea. With approximately 875,000 square feet (81,287 square meters)

of space dedicated to a new luxury hotel and marina, Nara Towers is a symbol not only of Beirut and its future; it will help to define that future by demonstrating the type of facilities needed in today's urban environments.

Situated on the shoreline of the Mediterranean Sea, the forty-seven-story tower is emphasized by its dramatic site. However, the sharp contrast between the tower's verticality and the landscape's horizontality is tempered by the organization of the complex, which is separated into two site-sensitive masses: the high rise is aligned with the straight edge of the coastal road, while the curved low rise conforms to the outline of a breakwater that encloses the marina. The multi-use program of the high- and low-rise buildings includes 327 guest-rooms and suites, restaurants, meeting rooms, a ballroom, a health club, and retail space.

Kingdom Centre

Architects	Ellerbe Becket, Minneapolis, Minnesota, USA
	Omrania Consortium, Riyadh, Saudi Arabia
Structural Engineer	Ove Arup & Partners
Client	HRH Prince Alwaleed bin Talal bin Abdulaziz Alsaud
Location	Riyadh, Saudi Arabia
Date	Estimated construction late 1997 – 2001

View of entry axis

Prince Alwaleed, grandson of King Abdulaziz, the founder of Saudi Arabia, wanted his Kingdom Centre to be a globally recognized icon of Riyadh and Saudi Arabia, just as the Eiffel Tower is a symbol for Paris and France. At 984 feet (300 meters), the same height as the Eiffel Tower, the Kingdom Centre is a distinctive focal point in Riyadh's skyline, where buildings average five stories and few exceed ten. As Riyadh's planning ordinance stipulates that buildings can have no more than thirty occupied floors, the top third of the Kingdom Centre is only sculptural, with the exception of the top level that functions as an observation deck.

To represent Saudi Arabia's role in the modern global economy, the Prince—very much involved in the design process—requested a simple, strong, monolithic, and symmetrical structure—a style more global than regional. Ellerbe Becket/Omrania Consortium's design was chosen from among more than one hundred competing proposals submitted by some of the world's top archi-

tectural firms over a span of three years. Their design consists of a slim tube that rises out of an elliptical floor plan and ends in a parabolic curve and shallow arch. The building is clad entirely in silver, reflective glass, concrete, granite, and brushed aluminum, materials which intensify its monolithic appearance.

The mixed-use tower accommodates different facilities, including the Prince's buisiness headquarters, a first-class hotel, the three-story Kingdom Mall, a wedding and conference center, rentable office space, a sports club, and luxury condominiums. To conform to Saudi customs and culture, a number of prayer rooms have been integrated into the layout, and one entire floor of the Kingdom Mall—reached by a separate entrance and elevator—is reserved for women only, where Islamic veils are not obligatory.

Opposite:
Model of
the complex

Section through Kingdom Mall

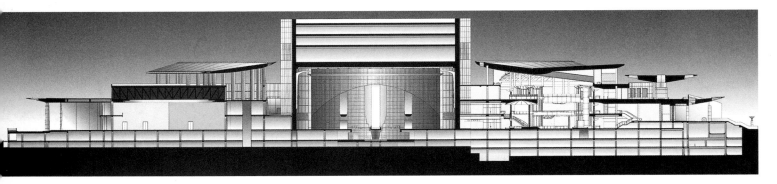

Emirates Twin Towers

Architect   NORR Limited, Toronto, Canada
NORR Group Consultants International Ltd., UAE

Structural Engineer   Hyder Consulting

Client   HH General Sheikh Mohammed bin Rashid al Maktoum

Location   Dubai, United Arab Emirates (UAE)

Date   Estimated construction June 1997 – Spring 2000

The towers under construction

Envisioned as a major landmark in the UAE's second largest city, Dubai, the Emirates Twin Tower project consists of a 1,154-foot (355-meter) high office tower and a 991-foot [305-meter] high hotel tower. Both high rises are connected by a low, horizontal, three-story podium that accommodates a skylit retail mall, the hotel's leisure areas, and underground service and parking facilities. The entire complex is set within a landscaped plaza featuring stainless-steel sculptural elements and fountains.

The nearly identical towers rise from an equilateral triangle plan. This Islamic-inspired, geometric pattern is repeated throughout the building, from sloped glass roofs and triangular skylights and canopy structures, to various interior and exterior paving designs. The rigid geometry is balanced by the curvilinear and terraced podium, which includes a cascading waterfall at the hotel entrance and circular glass drums which enclose the lower eight levels—an architectural motif that is repeated in the upper segments of the towers. The Twin Towers rise out of this granite base and are sheathed in aluminum and copper, reflective glass and metal, their slender proportions and glimmering material giving them widely visible profiles that sharply contrast with the predominantly arid surroundings.

The luxury hotel offers presidential suites and executive club rooms in the upper seven floors, and a fine restaurant, with panoramic views of the coastline, at the penthouse level. Two gently curved and terraced structures, reminiscent of massive sand dunes, embrace the complex at its east and west sides, providing further parking spaces.

In its contextual associations, the Emirates Twin Towers project represents a solution to the ongoing problem of how to combine contemporary technology and design with regional architectural forms and detailing.

Below and opposite:
The towers in
real and model form

Epilogue: The Elusive Dream

MARTHA THORNE

Introduction

Throughout the history of the skyscraper, the race for the tallest building in the world was dominated mostly by U.S. cities. Until relatively recently, one would have bet on either Chicago or New York to win the battle. Chicago's famous Home Insurance Building (1885) was 180 feet high (55 meters) with a skeletal iron framework inside its masonry walls to support the load. The Monadnock building (1891), at 216 feet (66 meters), is supported by masonry walls. However, the Park Row office building (1899) in New York City is supported by a steel frame and slightly taller than 380 feet (116 meters), making it the highest building of the nineteenth century. Subsequently New York City dominated the race during the early decades of the twentieth century: the 792-foot high (241 meter) Woolworth Building (1913) was the world's tallest for years until being superseded by the Chrysler Building in 1929. The Chrysler Building broke the 1,000-foot (305-meter) mark but was soon surpassed by the Empire State Building in 1931, which reigned as the world's tallest building for forty years.

Chicago presented a challenge on the residential front with its tall apartment buildings along the shores of Lake Michigan. A good example is Lake Point Tower (1968), which has seventy stories and is 645 feet (197 meters) high. Although the World Trade Center towers (1972) in lower Manhattan, each 110 stories high, established a new overall height record of 1,368 feet (417 meters), when it was completed, the Sears Tower in Chicago (1974), at 1,454 feet (443 meters), claimed the title of Tallest Building in the World. The tower retained its title until February 1996, when Cesar Pelli & Associates' eighty-eight-story, 1,476-foot (450-meter) Petronas Towers (see pp. 82-83) assumed the title. This new building in Kuala Lumpur marked a major geographic shift in the focal point of building activity.

In 1997 the Council on Tall Buildings, realizing that the competition was gearing up again, created four categories for measuring the heights of buildings: height to the structural or architectural top; height to the highest occupied floor; height to the top of the roof; and height to the top of the antenna. The Sears Tower occupies first place in categories two and three, the Petronas Towers is the winner of category one, and the World Trade Center towers win category four.

In spite of rising to new heights, the fascination with reaching previously unattainable goals still stimulates the minds of architects, engineers, developers, and the public in a way similar to that experienced decades ago. The ability to dream and propose ideas can occur anywhere in the world—from the Americas to Europe, the Middle East to Southeast Asia.

New architectural schemes are being publicized almost daily. Articles on the World Wide Web, in newspapers, glossy real estate brochures, and professional and technical journals often cite projects in the planning and design stages. Yet too often these proposals remain on the drawing board. The factors contributing to the difficulty in realizing a design are many. They range from macro-economic factors—issues beyond the reach of the developer of, and other professionals involved in, a given project—the property market, and difficulties in securing planning approval, to, at the far end of the spectrum, a lack of true intent on the part of the promoters of the idea. Rarely is the failure of a project due to a lack of technological possibilities.

When reviewing information on future contenders for the tallest building in the world award, one thing becomes clear: all use the phrase "the tallest" as their claim to fame. Presented here is a look at some dreams that have either not yet come to fruition or, as will be the case with many, may never be realized. As a tribute to the race for the highest, they are presented in order, from shortest to tallest.

Trump World Tower, New York, New York, USA

New York developer Donald Trump has boasted that the Trump World Tower (Fig. 1) will capture the title of the tallest residential building since it will rise 861 feet (262 meters), making it almost as tall as the observation deck of the Empire State Building. It is located across the street from the thirty-nine-story United Nations complex in Manhattan. In spite of public protests, the New York City Buildings Department approved a permit for the tower in April 1999. In order to undertake the con-

2
Coral Creek Partners, LLC and DMJM Keating Architects, Trango Tower, Denver, Colorado, USA, perspective rendering

struction of such a tall building, an anomaly in that part of the city, The Trump Organization purchased the air rights to several adjoining buildings, included a public plaza that will permit five additional stories, and has taken advantage of the existing zoning laws for high density, enacted years ago when a Second Avenue subway was a possibility. The building, with a footprint of 145 x 78 feet (44 x 24 meters), will be a simple, rectangular shaft clad in bronze-colored glass. Because the glazing is structural, exterior mullions will not be necessary, making the building even more sleek. Designed by Costas Kondylis & Associates, P. C. of New York City, the building will contain 376 luxury condominiums with floor-to-ceiling windows that maximize views. Already under construction, it may very well be the first new building to stake its claim on the tallest residential building in the world title.

Trango Tower, Denver, Colorado, USA

Taking its inspiration from the striking geological formation in the Himalayas, the 2,000-foot (610-meter) shear face known to serious

1   Costas Kondylis & Associates, P. C., Trump World Tower, photomontage

mountain climbers is the Trango Tower (Fig. 2). The proposed new structure is claimed to be the tallest building in the U.S. west of the Mississippi. The idea, initiated by Denver businessman W. Scott Moore, with a design concept by the Los Angeles architect Richard Keating of DMJM Keating Architects, is to build a tower slightly over 1,000 feet (305 meters) or eighty-six stories. The city of Denver has no height restrictions, but it does enact sunshine ordinances that could affect the project. In response to this concern, the tower would be wedge shaped and very thin, incorporating retail and conference facilities, a hotel, and residential units beginning at the forty-first floor. The base is to be clad in honed and polished granite and the shaft in ochre-colored, striated stone and dark glass strips. Although no specific schedule has yet been set, the developer looks optimistically towards 2004.

Scandinavian Tower, Malmö, Sweden

Arthur Buchardt and the Øyer Invest AS Company are promoting a circular tower approximately 90 feet (27 meters) in diameter and 1,065 feet (325 meters) in height (Fig. 3), which will be twice the height of the tallest building in Scandinavia, a hotel in Oslo. The proposal includes a 700-room hotel, a casino, and conference facilities, making the tower a place to showcase Scandinavian products and services with a view towards trade. It is hoped to become a transportation crossroads—serving both Denmark and Sweden—when the high-speed rail link is completed. The building is an enormous column of glowing light that juts northward at its tip. Whether or not construction will proceed depends on achieving a consensus between investors, the public, and the Malmö community.

3
Wingårdh Arkitektkontor AB,
Scandinavian Tower,
Malmö, Sweden,
view of model

Jakarta Tower, Jakarta, Indonesia

French architect Jean-Paul Viguier has designed what he hopes will be a new landmark for the city—if it is built and attains the projected height of 1,186 feet (361 meters). The slender, circular tower, less than 150 feet (46 meters) in diameter, is composed of five, twenty-five-story modules—which look like Dixie cups stacked on top of one another—separated from each other by spacious sky lobbies (Fig. 4). Each module has an open central core that facilitates the entry of natural light into the interior. Gardens are proposed for the central atriums, and the project will house below-ground parking and residences, offices, a hotel, and other amenities above ground. Four vertical columns, which are linked horizontally at each sky lobby, will support the building. The architect's 1995 proposal remains in the concept stage.

Tour San Fins, Paris, France

In 1988 French architect Jean Nouvel began designing the Tour Sans Fins for Paris. It was

4   Jean Paul Viguier,
Jakarta Tower,
Jakarta, Indonesia,
view of model

5 M3 Architects, Citygate
Ecotower, London, UK,
computer rendering

6 Haines Lundberg Waehler,
Chongqing Office Tower,
Sichuan, China, conceptual
perspective rendering

the winning entry in a design competition for a site next to the Grande Arche (Otto von Spreckelsen, 1989) in the La Défense area of the city. Projected at one hundred levels and 1,397 feet (426 meters) high, the building was to be a circular, glass tower that became more transparent the higher it rose. Beginning with polished black granite at its base, it would move into gray granite, then aluminum, then polished stainless steel, semi-reflecting glass, and, finally, clear glass at its top, through which the pendular damping system would be visible. Although the office tower was designed and feasibility and financial studies were positive, the economic recession of the late eighties halted the project.

Citygate Ecotower, London, England

The London firm of M3 Architects has initiated a theoretical proposal for a tall but ecologically sound tower (Fig. 5). The project's principals, Ken Hutt and Nadi Jahangiri, had worked together previously on the London Millennium Tower (p. 127) and Commerzbank, Frankfurt/Main, Germany (pp. 110-111), with Foster and Partners.

The 1,495-foot (456-meter) high building is intended for mixed uses that include transport interchange, offices, and residential accommodations. The suggested site is along the eastern approach to London. The firm states that it seeks to unite its interest in the high-rise type with low energy building design. The tower, which resembles a great sail, includes wind slots which prevent turbulence at its base and harness the wind to drive turbines—which coupled with 50% photovoltaic cell coverage of the facade provide up to half of the overall power consumption of the building. A three-story, ventilated facade section eliminates the need for conventional air-conditioning systems.

World Center for Vedic Learning, Madhya Pradesh, India

In 1998 it was announced that the tallest building in the world would be constructed in Madhya Pradesh, India. Intended by Maharishi Mahesh Yogi, the spiritual leader of the sect, to be the global center of Vedic learning, and thus designed according to the laws of the religion, the new building was to be a giant temple of Vedic proportions, decorated with traditional elements. The Center was to be 2,222 feet high (677 meters), 1,111 feet (339 meters) on each side of its square base, and to have livable space on 144 floors.

A similar tower in São Paulo, Brazil was announced the following year in a July issue of *The New York Times*. The overall concept was to be inspired by Vedic principles but suited to the climate, technology, and economics of its South American location. The building would be multifunctional, 103 stories, or 1,622 feet (494 meters) high, and contain hotels, offices, a convention center, and university. The Maharishi Global Development fund was to be the main investor in the project, along with Brazilian businessman Mario Garnero. The unconventional design, as well as that of the World Learning Center, is to be undertaken by the U.S. firm of Yamasaki Associates, architects of the World Trade Center in New York City.

Chongqing Office Tower, Sichuan, People's Republic of China

On a site in the center of old downtown Chongqing, Sichuan, China, a building with a minimum of one hundred stories is proposed for commercial, office, and hotel uses (Fig. 6). The firm of HLW was commissioned by the Chongqing National Garden City, Inc. to act as the development manager for the project. HLW will head up a team to undertake the entire project in a turnkey fashion, from design to building management. Originally planned to be completed before the end of this century, the project is currently on hold due to economic constraints.

The building will have a gross surface of over 2.5 million square feet (232,250 square meters) and rise to a height of 1,693 feet (516 meters). The eight-story lobby will be the main commercial and pedestrian section of the project. Offices will extend from the eighth to the eightieth floor; on top of these floors will be a hotel through floor 105. Mechanical systems and observation levels will occupy the rest of the building to the 114th floor. The top of the building is designed to reference traditional Chinese imagery. The cubic form of the observatory levels represents "temples," or scholarly retreats, which are "perched" on top of the tower. Antennas for telecommunication purposes will eventually crown the building. In regard to the building's structure, engineers are considering either a forty-eight-column, steel perimeter tube scheme with a light steel core or a cast-in-place concrete, perimeter frame with a concrete core.

Project X, Pusan, South Korea

The prolific Japanese architect, Kisho Kurokawa, is designing a skyscraper for the city of Pusan in South Korea that will prove to be taller than Petronas Towers. Project X (Fig. 7) will incorporate a number of structural innovations that will allow it to withstand earthquakes and extreme winds. The building is designed like a basket, with a central core and a peripheral zone with short-span columns. The superstructure and ordinary structure will

be synthesized as one, single structure. The superstructure will consist of two-floor trusses positioned approximately every 160 feet (49 meters). At each juncture, a computer-operated, anti-seismic system will create a force that opposes seismic vibrations, thereby protecting the building from dangerous horizontal movements. With the slowing of South Korea's economy during the mid-1990s, the timetable for this project has also slowed.

Grollo Tower, Melbourne, Australia

Melbourne, Australia will be the site of the world's tallest skyscraper if developer Bruno Grollo can achieve the goal he once stated: "The Grollo Tower is the landmark Melbourne has needed for decades. . . . We have a seductively beautiful design, the world's most livable city desperately looking for an international

7 Kisho Kurokawa Architect and Associates, Project X, Pusan, South Korea, computer rendering

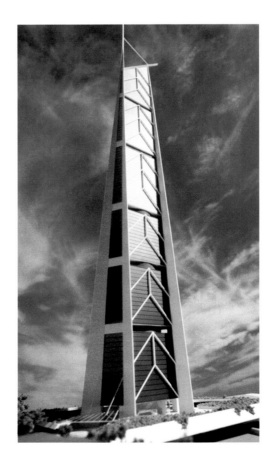

8
Harry Seidler and Associates, Grollo Tower, Melbourne, Australia, computer-rendered perspective

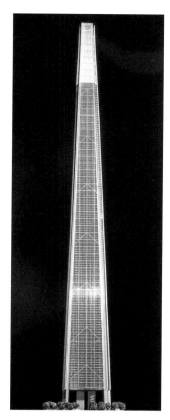

9 Denton Corker Marshall, Grollo Tower, Melbourne, Australia, model

landmark, a centrally located wasteland, the technological skills, the confidence, and the vision to make it happen."

Architect Harry Seidler unveiled his design for the tower in May 1995. His 1,625-foot (495-meter) hexagonal tower had a tapered profile supported by only six exterior columns and a triangular central core—which helped carry the vertical load for the lower section of the building (Fig. 8). His concept was to locate the tower on a large podium, possibly on a site over an old railyard, thereby affording dramatic views in all directions. The application of solar technology was fundamental to Seidler's concept: photovoltaic cells were to be embedded in the facade's glazing to convert a substantial part of the solar radiation into electric energy.

Due to a lukewarm public and governmental response to the original design, developer

Bruno Grollo commissioned a second design for a specific site in the Docklands area of Melbourne. For the second scheme, he chose the Australian firm of Denton Corker Marshall. Their proposal is a glass, multi-use obelisk, 113 stories—or 1,820 feet (555 meters)—high, containing shops, offices, apartments, and a hotel (Fig. 9). The basic structural elements are four pairs of columns that raise the tower off the ground, creating space for a park more than 100 feet (30 meters) high at its ground level and the symmetrical central core which contains circulation and services. The building has three main parts, each separated by a triple-level sky lobby. Above the top, or hotel section, are observation decks, a restaurant, shops, and recreational facilities. The uppermost 350 feet (107 meters) is the "Light Pinnacle," a beacon filled with telecommunications equipment and capped with an open viewing platform. The structural system, visible through the glass skin of the building, consists of "ladders," diagonal bracing trusses at selected intervals which transfer loads to the paired corner columns, each of which rest on an independent pad at bedrock level.

The plans won government approval in December 1998 but were subject to financing within a four-month time frame. In early 1999, the planned development was scrapped when it became apparent that the gap between the twenty million Australian dollars offered by the developers and the thirty-seven million Australian dollars required by the Docklands Authority—the body entrusted with the overall redevelopment of the area—could not be bridged.

Millennium Tower, London, England

In 1996 Foster and Partners unveiled a scheme for a 1,265-foot (386-meter) tower in London

10
Foster and Partners,
Millennium Tower,
London, England,
photomontage

(Fig. 10). The 1.5 million square feet (139,350 square meters) of usable space, promoted by the Norwegian-based business group, Kvaerner, would provide a landmark space in which to secure London's preeminence as the financial capital of Europe. The mixed-use complex would serve approximately 8,000 people with offices, apartments, shops, and amenities that would include a public viewing gallery at 1,000 feet (305 meters). The unusual, free-form plan meant that the building's appearance would change as light reflected off its curved, glass facade. Therefore, the top of the building would divide into two tail fins of differing heights, solving the problem of how to elegantly finish the building's top.

The proposed elevator system, which would be among the fastest in the world, would travel at almost 30 feet (9.1 meters) per second. The double-deck cars could distribute passengers to "sky-lobbies" located throughout the building. In order to minimize movement of the tower in wind, a Tuned Mass Damping (TMD) system would be located at the top of the structure. When the building moves, a pad would move an equal distance in the opposite direction, slowing the building down.

The architects also proposed a series of bio-climatic measures to reduce the enormous amounts of energy a tall building usually requires. These include sky parks to provide shade for the building, cooling systems supplemented by natural ventilation, and blinds. The project may also rely on a cold water aquifer, 200 feet (61 meters) below ground, to cool its heating system. The future of this project is uncertain since obtaining the approval for it is a cumbersome procedure in London, and the first proposals were rejected in their original form.

7 South Dearborn Street, Chicago, Illinois, USA

A proposal for the heart of downtown Chicago, initiated by European-American Realty Ltd., aims to put the city again in the running for the world's tallest building. The mixed-use building will measure 2,000 feet (610 meters) in height including its antenna (Fig. 11), and include a retail concourse, thirteen floors of parking, approximately thirty stories of offices, 350 residential units on forty-two floors, and communications levels.

The Chicago office of Skidmore, Owings & Merrill is designing the building which is a sleek, rectangular, steel-and-glass tower with curved corners, divided into six sections, which step back as the building rises. The entire top section is devoted to communications floors, mechanical systems, a cooling tower, and the Tuned Mass Damping system. Its height, the maximum allowed by the Federal Aviation Administration without special approval, will meet the increasing future demands of digital television broadcasting systems. The tower is constructed of a concrete tube structure, which forms the spine from which floors cantilever out twenty to thirty feet (six to nine meters). This means that the upper residential floors have no perimeter columns dividing the space, and the lower office floors have open plans with additional support provided by external columns.

Millennium Tower, Tokyo, Japan

Designed by Foster and Partners (architects) and Ove Arup & Partners (structural engineers) for the Obayashi Corporation, the proposed 170-story, multi-use high rise (Fig. 12), if constructed, will reach 2,755 feet (840 meters),

11 Skidmore, Owings & Merrill, 7 South Dearborn Street, Chicago, Illinois, USA, view of model

12 Foster and Partners,
Millennium Tower, Tokyo,
Japan, model

almost twice the height of the Sears Tower. The tower will easily overshadow all other skyscrapers from its offshore site in Tokyo Bay. Using a helical steel cage, woven like a basket, the Millennium Tower has a conical shape that offers both an aesthetic and structural solution to the design limits of the very tall building. In laboratory studies, the conical shape proved the most stable, since potentially destabilizing winds move safely around the building's contours.

Construction, which is expected to take ten years to complete, involves the use of an all-weather "construction plant" that will erect and weld together the central core. The perimeter steelwork will be constructed with the use of cranes. Other technological innovations planned for the tower include double-deck elevators that can transport up to 160 people at a time to sky centers every thirty floors, from which points passengers may continue their ascent via local lifts.

The Race Continues

The skyscraper, the twentieth-century building type par excellence, has been called a magnifying glass through which we may observe our society. This building type is one of the most significant innovations in building technology in the last one hundred years. From Art Deco, Modernism, and Postmodernism to the present search for new forms of expression, an analysis of the history of tall buildings illustrates general shifts in style and aesthetic concerns in the field of architecture. The similarity of

tall buildings built in both the East and West today signals that our world is becoming smaller and more interrelated. Major construction activity has shifted from Chicago and New York to Asia, reflecting changes in economics, politics, and society.

No doubt the infatuation with height will continue without limits, some projects literally inching ahead into first place, if only for a matter of months. Fantastic proposals will continue to be drawn, in the spirit of Frank Lloyd Wright's Mile High Illinois, a tower he designed for Chicago in 1956. These inventions will push the limits of our thinking and encourage new directions for research and exploration. The factors influencing whether or not to build include economics, supply and demand, land availability, construction costs, zoning ordinances, air rights, and even airplane flight paths. But that is not all. The desire to build "the tallest" is, and will continue to be, a motivating factor. The challenge to rise to new heights, to break existing records, and to make a statement beyond the realm of necessity will continue to inspire architects, engineers, and promoters of buildings.

It is clear that the buildings mentioned herein form only a partial list of dynamic, unrealized projects. Every day new ideas and proposals are initiated that aspire to be the tallest. However, if true progress is to be made, it seems that the question should not be one of title alone. Height should be evaluated alongside architectural quality and a building's contribution to the quality of life.

Biographies of Architects and Firms

Arquitectonica

In his introduction to a catalogue of Arquitectonica's work, Frederick Koeper writes that "... Miami is recognized for its association with Arquitectonica, a firm whose unmistakable style, distinguished by high-spirited and unambiguous forms set off in brilliant colors, has created landmarks along Biscayne Bay." Among the most recognizable of these landmarks is the Atlantis (1980-82), a building popularized by its weekly appearance in the opening sequence of the television series *Miami Vice*. Although it has now been nearly twenty years since the condominium building was constructed, the Atlantis exhibits several of the formal and material elements associated with Arquitectonica's work, including the use of a High Modernist steel-and-glass grid enlivened by strong color and an element of the unexpected, such as the large cube of space that dramatically punctures the building's center.

Today, Arquitectonica has expanded its presence beyond Miami and has offices in Asia, Europe, and North and South America. The firm is headed by the husband-and-wife team of Bernardo Fort-Brescia and Laurinda Spear, who were two of the firm's founding principals in 1977. Born in Lima, Peru, Fort-Brescia received his bachelor's degree in architecture and urban planning from Princeton University in 1973 and his master's degree in architecture from Harvard University in 1975. Born in Miami, Florida, Spear received her bachelor's degree in fine arts from Brown University in 1972 and her master's degree in architecture from Columbia University in 1975. She was also the recipient of the Rome Prize for Architecture in 1978.

Ricardo Bofill, Taller de Arquitectura

Born in Barcelona in 1939, Ricardo Bofill studied at the Escuela Tecnica Superior de Arquitectura in Barcelona from 1955 to 1956 as well as at the University of Geneva from 1957 to 1960. In 1961 Bofill founded the Taller de Arquitectura (Architectural Workshop), which continues to maintain offices in Barcelona and Paris. Throughout the workshop's history, members have included not only architects and engineers but also mathematicians, musicians, philosophers, and sociologists. In the language of Postmodernism, Bofill explains that the workshop's multidisciplinary approach is necessary "to confront the complexity of architectural practice."

In opposition to what have been critiqued as the ahistorical and antihumanist designs of High Modernism, Taller de Arquitectura's works are grounded in today's cultural and historical context. The workshop's interest in contextualism is characteristically expressed by the appropriation of a classical vocabulary, as illustrated in the skyscraper at 77 West Wacker Drive in Chicago, which includes a gridded facade of columns crowned with four pediments. However, the workshop has had other directions in the past, including an interest in the vernacular forms of the Mediterranean. The workshop's stylistic transformations are attributable to its rigorous reevaluation of how design produces meaningful environments.

Brennan Beer Gorman/Architects

Based in New York, Brennan Beer Gorman/Architects also have offices in Washington, D.C. and Hong Kong. Established in 1984 by Hank Brennan, David Beer, and Peter Gorman, the firm specializes in the design of office buildings and interiors as well as other commercial building types. Peter Gorman and Yann LeRoy were the project architects for the Jakarta Stock Exchange Building (see pp. 72-73). Underlying each project—whether dedicated to business, hospitality, or retail—is an "efficient and flexible design solution." Within the parameters of their pragmatic approach, the firm works to "push the design expression [of each building] toward new horizons." Expressive gestures may be revealed in massing, as in the Jakarta Financial Tower's profile

Bernardo Fort-Brescia and Laurinda Spear

Ricardo Bofill

Peter Gorman

which echoes the shape of ship's bow, or in materials, as in the Sofitel, New York, where limestone is juxtaposed dramatically with curved bands of glass.

With projects in Europe, Mexico, the Middle East, Southeast Asia, and South America, Brennan Beer Gorman has an international presence. The firm also has projects in Eastern Europe with partner Frank LaSusa, a member—the first from America—of Russia's most prestigious architectural organization, the Moscow Union of Architects.

Busby + Associates Architects

Born in 1952, Peter Busby received his bachelor of arts degree from the University of Toronto in 1974 and his master's degree in architecture from the University of British Columbia in 1977. Busby founded his Vancouver-based firm in 1984. The firm was later restructured as Busby + Associates to reflect the important contributions of associate architects Michael Elkan, Brian Ellis, Susan Gushe, Jim Hoffman, Mike McColl, Teryl Mullock, and Brent Welty. Busby is one of Vancouver's most prominent firms, and their projects have ranged from the very small—a mobile cappuccino kiosk (1984)—to the very large—the Sheraton Tower at Wall Centre (1998-2001; see pp. 18-19).

Busby + Associates are committed to "design excellence," which the firm closely associates with the use of advanced technology. Their interest in providing "leading edge environmental solutions" no doubt reflects Peter Busby's three-year position as project architect for Foster and Partners, a firm famous for its innovative application of technology in environmentally sensitive buildings. Busby + Associates transform their desire to design comfortable and convenient environments into elegantly detailed buildings characterized by extensive glazing which bathes their interiors in natural light.

Peter Busby

Clockwise from top left: Greg Carpenter, William Karst, John Malone, and Spencer Johnson

Callison Architecture

Based in Seattle, Callison Architecture aims to be "the preferred architectural firm for business leaders worldwide." Initial steps towards achieving this goal were taken when the firm's founder, Anthony Callison, received a commission from the luxury retailer Nordstrom in 1975. Like Nordstrom, a company distinguished by attention to customer service, Callison Architecture is dedicated to "uncompromising service and customer satisfaction." Today, the firm specializes in corporate, health care, hospitality, and retail design, and their clients include some of the most important companies in these fields, including Eddie Bauer, Hewlett-Packard, Microsoft, Nike, and the Sisters of Providence.

With over 400 employees, Callison Architecture is one of the largest architectural firms in the United States. Its success with corporate clients at home has been exported abroad, and the firm now has projects in China, Japan, Latin America, and the Middle East for clients such as the Bank of China and Seibu Department Stores of Japan. Team members of the Grand Gateway at Xu Jia Hui (see pp. 58-59) include Designer Greg Carpenter, Principal-in-Charge William Karst, Project Manager John Malones, and Master Planner Spencer Johnson.

Coop Himmelb(l)au

Based in Vienna, Coop Himmelb(l)au was established by Wolf D. Prix, Helmut Swiczkinsky, and Rainer Michael Holzer—who left in 1971—in 1968.

In 1988 the firm opened a second office in Los Angeles.

Born in 1942 in Vienna, Wolf D. Prix was educated at the Technical University of Vienna, the Southern California Institute of Architecture in Los Angeles, and the Architectural Association in London. In addition to his architectural practice, Prix is a professor at the University of Applied Arts in Vienna, an adjunct professor at the Southern California Institute of Architects, and a faculty member of Columbia University in New York City. Helmut Swiczinsky was born in Poznan, Poland in 1944 and raised in Vienna. Like Prix, he was educated at the Technical University of Vienna and the Architectural Association in London. Their firm is famous for its avant-garde designs, which have been widely exhibited in shows including Philip Johnson's landmark *Deconstructivist Architecture* exhibition at the Museum of Modern Art.

Helmut Swiczinsky (left) and Wolf D. Prix (right)
Photo © Gerald Zugmann

Denton Corker Marshall

Based in Melbourne, Australia, Denton Corker Marshall was established by John Denton, Bill Corker, and Barrie Marshall in 1972. Today, James Gibson, Budiman Hendropurnomo, Richard Johnson, Adrian Pilton, and Jeff Walker are also directors. Winner of the Royal Australian Institute of Architects' gold medal in 1996, Denton Corker Marshall is one of Australia's most lauded firms.

From left to right: Jeff Walker, Adrian Pilton, and Richard Johnson

In a review for *Architecture Australia* (May–June 1996), Anthony Styant-Browne credited the firm's "extraordinary success" to its collaborative design approach, which "produces better, more profound, more rigorous work than any of the individuals could produce alone."

Architectural critics invariably characterize the firm's work as challenging and intellectual. Like many other architectural firms, Denton Corker Marshall design high-rise offices, hotels, and shopping centers. However, in contrast to the blandness of most commercial architecture, Denton Corker Marshall's buildings visually impact the built landscape, through either dramatic formal gestures, such as the dynamic diagonal of the Melbourne Exhibition Centre's canopy, or through expressive contrasts in material, such as the steel armature and reflective glass walls of the 222 Exhibition Street Office Building in Melbourne.

Although Denton Corker Marshall's buildings are perhaps most visible in Melbourne and Sydney, the firm's international practice includes offices in Hong Kong, Indonesia, Poland, Vietnam, and the United Kingdom. Their foreign projects include the Coca Cola Bottling Plant in Sha Tin, Hong Kong, the Segitiga Senen Shopping Centre in Jakarta, Indonesia, and Saigon Centre in Ho Chi Minh City, Vietnam.

Ellerbe Becket/Omrania Consortium

Ellerbe Becket is one of the oldest and largest design firms in the United States. In nine decades, the firm has designed nearly every major building type in all fifty states and many foreign countries. The firm has more than 800 employees in twelve offices worldwide. Omrania & Associates is one of the leading architecture and engineering firms in Saudi Arabia.

Ellerbe Becket's Kingdom Centre (see pp. 118-119) team was a large, interdisciplinary group including AIA Design Principals Rich Varda and Scott Berry, and AIA Managing Principal William Chilton, who worked in close collaboration with Omrania's principal, Basem Al-Shihabi.

Varda received a bachelor of science in landscape architecture from the University of Wisconsin and a master of architecture from the University of Minnesota. Berry received a bachelor of architecture from the University of Minnesota. Chilton received a bachelor of arts in architecture from Iowa State University and a master of architecture from the University of Minnesota. Al-Shihabi received a bachelor of science in architecture from the University of Minnesota and a post-graduate diploma in landscape architecture from the University of Edinburgh.

Foster and Partners

Born in Manchester in 1935, Norman Foster was educated at the University of Manchester School of Architecture and Department of Town and Country Planning from 1956 to 1961 as well as the Yale University School of Architecture from 1961 to 1962. In 1967 Foster established his private practice in London. One of the most highly esteemed architects of the late twentieth century, Foster was knighted in the Queen's Honours List in 1990 and became Lord Foster in 1999. He has also been the recipient of numerous awards, including the prestigious Royal Gold Medal (1983), the AIA Gold Medal (1994), and the Pritzker Prize (1999).

Norman Foster is well known as the designer of airports, museums, and train stations, including London's Third Airport at Stansted, the Carré d'Art in Nîmes, France, and the Bilbao Metro System in Spain. However, he is perhaps more famous for two high-profile skyscrapers: the Hongkong and Shanghai Banking Corporation Hong Kong Headquarters (1981-85) and the Commerzbank Headquarters (see pp. 110-111) in Frankfurt/Main (1991-97). Rather than design buildings according to convention, Foster "go[es] back to basics . . . to understand the underlying principles of a problem in order to question the traditional response and identify if there is an opportunity to invent or reinvent a solution." It is not an inexpensive approach: the custom-designed Hongkong and Shanghai Banking Corporation Hong Kong Headquarters is reportedly the most costly building ever constructed. However, the results are impressive. In the Hongkong and Shanghai Banking Corporation Hong Kong Headquarters, Foster revolutionized both the physical and social environment of the tall office building. By incorporating escalators, rather than elevators, as the main mode of vertical circulation, the building's core is open to air and light. The use of escalators also facilitates social interaction much more successfully than the confined interior of the standard elevator.

Norman Foster

Fox & Fowle Architects, P. C.

Based in New York City, Fox & Fowle Architects was founded by Robert F. Fox, Jr. and Bruce S. Fowle in 1978. Born in White Plains, New York in 1941, Fox received his bachelor's degree in architecture from Cornell and his master's degree in architecture from Harvard University. Fowle, who was born in Flushing, New York in 1937, received his bachelor's degree in architecture from Syracuse University in 1960. Today, the fifty-five-person firm includes three additional principals: Michael R. Franck, who is the director of the interiors studio; Daniel J. Kaplan, who is the director of high-rise and mixed-use projects; and Sylvia J. Smith, who is the director of institutional projects.

Bruce S. Fowle

American Institute of Architects Fellow Bruce S. Fowle directs the firm's design, which is strongly influenced by his interest in sustainable architecture. Fowle's commitment to environmentally responsible architecture results in buildings designed with sustainable materials using ecologically sensitive processes. Energy conservation is also a design priority, as is the maintenance of natural light and quality air conditions. Fox & Fowle's design approach thereby ensures that both the interiors and exteriors of their buildings are environmentally sensitive. Such concerns are especially important considering the impact buildings can have on the health of their occupants. Fox & Fowle's use of individual air handling units and oversized, outside air shafts in buildings like The Condé Nast Building at Four Times Square (pp. 36-37) help circumvent conditions that cause "sick building syndrome," which has afflicted many tenants of poorly ventilated buildings. Fox & Fowle encourages the daily implementation of green principles among its staff by providing regular in-house training sessions.

Michael Graves & Associates

Born in Indianapolis in 1934, Michael Graves received his bachelor's degree in architecture from the University of Cincinnati in 1958 and his master's degree in architecture from Harvard University in 1959. From 1960 to 1962, he studied at the American Academy in Rome, where he was a recipient of the Rome Prize and the Brunner Fellowship. Returning from Rome, Graves embarked on a career as both an architect and a teacher. Currently the Robert Schirmer Professor of Architecture at Princeton, he has taught at the university since 1962.

Since his association with the famed 1960s architecture group the New York Five, Graves has been one of the most highly profiled contemporary architects practicing in the United States. His projects, which include The Portland Building in Oregon (1983) and Walt Disney World's Dolphin and Swan Hotels in Florida (1987), are icons of postmodern architecture. Graves has expanded the audience for his designs with a collection of household products for the Italian firm Alessi and the popular American retailer Target.

Michael Graves

T. R. Hamzah & Yeang Sdn Bhd

Based in Kuala Lumpur, Tengku Robert Hamzah and Ken Yeang founded T. R. Hamzah & Yeang in 1976. Hamzah and Yeang's sixty-six-person firm now also operates offices in Australia, China, and Singapore. Both partners were educated in England, as is common in Malaysia where American architecture credentials are not accepted. Dr. Yeang is a graduate of the Architectural Association School in London and he received his doctoral degree from Cambridge University.

As well known for his writings as for his buildings, Dr. Yeang is the author of several influential books, including *Designing with Nature* and *The Skyscraper: Bioclimatically Considered.* A specialist in the design of bioclimatic, or ecologically sustainable, skyscrapers, Dr. Yeang seeks "to build with minimal impact on the natural

Ken Yeang

environment and to integrate the built environment with the ecological systems (ecosystems) of the locality." Dr. Yeang concedes that "Skyscrapers . . . are by all means and purposes not low-energy or self-evident ecological buildings." However, he notes that "the skyscraper as a building type shall continue to be in existence in most of the world's cities . . . for at least the next decade or so." Consequently, Dr. Yeang's strategy is to minimize the impact of his buildings by limiting their energy consumption, often by appropriating vernacular design approaches. The firm has been recognized for its bioclimatic skyscrapers with both a Royal Australian Institute of Architects' International Architecture Award (1996) and a Citation from the American Institute of Architects (1996) for its twelve-story Menara Mesiniaga building in Malaysia.

Hijjas Kasturi Associates

Based in Kuala Lumpur, Hijjas Kasturi Associates was founded by Singapore-born architect Hijjas bin Kasturi in 1977. Kasturi received his architectural education in Australia under the Colombo Plan for Co-Operative Economic and Social Development in Asia and the Pacific, which was established at the Commonwealth Conference of Foreign Affairs in January 1950.

Hijjas bin Kasturi

Hijjas Kasturi Associates' early commissions were typically "community based" buildings such as hospitals and schools. The firm now also designs commercial and industrial structures and was, in fact, a forerunner in the economic use of prefabricated construction in Malaysia, where the standard construction method is in-situ concrete for commercial and industrial buildings.

Hijjas bin Kasturi's architecture reflects an interest in the history of Malaysian design; however, he avoids the literal quotation of architectural forms commonly associated with Postmodernism, explaining that the "[l]iteral transposition from the traditional is not possible without responding to specific problems and opportunities."

Ingenhoven Overdiek und Partner

Based in Düsseldorf, Germany, Ingenhoven Overdiek und Partner was founded by Christoph Ingenhoven and Jürgen Overdiek in 1993. With approximately eighty-five employees, the firm includes architects, engineers, graphic designers, industrial designers, interior designers, and model makers.

Ingenhoven Overdiek und Partner specialize in the design of high rises and other types of commercial buildings. Characteristic of German architectural firms, Ingenhoven Overdiek und Partner emphasize the importance of environmentally sensitive design, which minimizes the impact of buildings on their surroundings by incorporating ecological materials and methods of construction. The firm is equally concerned about the interior environments of their buildings. Christoph Ingenhoven writes that "good buildings make it possible to free ourselves from the dependence created by automated technology," demonstrating his belief that natural ventilation is superior to that provided by technologically advanced heating and air-conditioning systems.

Christoph Ingenhoven

Likewise, Ingenhoven observes that "There is no substitute for daylight." Consequently, Ingenhoven Overdiek und Partner's buildings are characterized by extensive glazing that allows for both the natural light and ventilation that the firm so strongly values.

Kaplan McLaughlin Diaz

Based in San Francisco, Kaplan McLaughlin Diaz was founded by Ellis Kaplan, Herbert McLaughlin, and James Diaz in 1963. Today, Mohinder Datta is one of the principals, replacing Ellis Kaplan who is no longer with the firm. Herbert McLaughlin was the director of design of the Nadya Park International Design Center and Corporate Office Tower (see pp. 74-75). McLaughlin, who was born in Chicago in 1934, received both his bachelor of arts degree and his master of architecture degree from Yale University.

Herbert McLaughlin

Kaplan McLaughlin Diaz consists of approximately 150 employees who work in the firm's national offices in Los Angeles, New York, Portland, and Seattle, as well as in its international offices in Mexico City, Mexico and Tokyo, Japan. The firm designs a variety of commercial structures, including health care, hotel, office, and retail buildings. The firm also has received a significant number of commissions from city, county, and state governments to design court facilities. Examples of the firm's state-of-the-art buildings include the Oakland Federal Building, the San Mateo County Municipal Court Building, and the California State Supreme Court Building. The firm's great variety of design approaches reflects its vision of each project as "unique and calling for a special solution." However, underlying KMD's various designs is a dedication to creating a special sense of place for each of their building's users.

Kohn Pedersen Fox Associates, P. C.

Based in New York City, Kohn Pedersen Fox Associates was founded by A. Eugene Kohn, William Pedersen, and Sheldon Fox in 1976. The firm has designed a seemingly unlimited number of building types, including museums, hotels, and residences as well as educational, entertainment, health care, institutional, retail, and transportation facilities. However, as Christian Norberg-Schultz has noted, "Like no other architectural firm, Kohn Pedersen Fox has dedicated its attention to the development of the most characteristic and significant American building type, the skyscraper." The firm's special attention to the tall building has merited principal William Pedersen two National Honor Awards from the American Institute of Architects—for the skyscraper at 333 Wacker Drive in Chicago (1984) and the Westendstrasse 1/DG Bank Headquarters in Frankfurt/Main, Germany (1995). Pedersen was educated at the University of Minnesota, where he received his bachelor's degree in architecture in 1961, and the Massachusetts Institute of Technology, where he received his master's degree in architecture as a Whitney Fellow in 1963. He has worked in collaboration with Joshua Chaiken on the Shanghai World Financial Center and with Douglas Hocking and Jerri Smith on the Portland Federal Courthouse (see pp. 30-31).

Kohn Pedersen Fox states that it "does not have any one, specific architectural style." In fact, formal differences between the firm's designs—which range from the rectilinear, masonry clad 225 West Wacker Drive to its curved, curtain-walled neighbor at 333 West Wacker Drive, both located in Chicago—demonstrate a variety of stylistic approaches. However, the firm's interest in context, as well as its willingness to organize a building's massing according to local conditions, indicates its interest in issues associated with postmodern architecture. Kohn Pedersen Fox's postmodern philosophy is further revealed by

From left to right: Jerri Smith, Douglas Hocking, and William Pedersen. Photo © Siobhan M. Lowe

William Pedersen's wish to design buildings that "acknowledge not only the past, but also the present and the future . . . that attempt to combine simultaneously the formal with the informal, the figural with the abstract, the monumental with the human, and the modern with the traditional."

Architekten Kollhoff & Timmermann

In his preface to *The New German Architecture*, Gerhardt G. Feldmeyer writes that architecture in "[t]he 1990s appear[s] to belong to Germany." Feldmeyer lists Architekten Kollhoff & Timmermann as one of the firms that has increased the profile of German architecture in the late twentieth century. Born in Lobenstein in 1946, Hans Kollhoff received his bachelor's degree in architecture from Karlsruhe University in 1975 and his master's degree in architecture from Cornell University in 1978. Following his graduation, Kollhoff was in private practice until 1984, when he established the Berlin-based firm Architekten Kollhoff & Timmermann with Helga Timmermann.

With their country's reunification, German architects have been afforded the opportunity, and the challenge, to build in former East Germany, where there had been little construction since the end of World War II. In November 1990, the German Architecture Museum and the *Frankfurter Allgemeine* newspaper sponsored a competition to redesign the Potsdamer Platz in the center of Berlin. Kollhoff received considerable attention for his proposal, which he designed in collaboration with Norbert Hemprich. Explaining his design, which included a collection of high-rise commercial and residential buildings, Kollhoff explained that "Although we wish to give the square its historical design back, we do not believe that this can be achieved by a restoration that tries to remain true to the original, nor by a pluralist modernity." Kollhoff thereby distinguished his approach from that characteristically associated with Postmodernism, offering instead what Manfred Sack has described as "a fine sensibility towards the classical roots of modernism."

Lucien Lagrange and Associates

As a recent *Wall Street Journal* article on Chicago architecture reported, "A building boom is beginning to erupt here . . . creating opportunities for a new generation of talented designers" in large part because "[t]he city's most famous architects—Helmut Jahn, Adrian Smith and Dirk Lohan—are focused mainly overseas" (July 8, 1998). One of

Lucien Lagrange

Dennis Lau

the smaller firms that has most benefited from the increase in construction is Lucien Lagrange and Associates, a thirty-three-person firm founded in 1985.

Born in 1940 in France and educated at McGill University in Canada, Lucien Lagrange began his career at Skidmore, Owings & Merrill in 1978, where he quickly rose from senior designer to studio head to associate partner. During his seven-year tenure at Skidmore, Owings & Merrill, Lagrange designed, among other things, the Dearborn Park residential complex (phase one: 1974-77; phase two: 1979-87)—a veritable "suburb in the city"—and One Financial Place (1985), whose presence helped to revitalize the once depressed area of Chicago's south loop.

When he left Skidmore, Owings & Merrill in the 1980s, Lagrange's practice was limited to small commissions. Today, his firm's projects include what the *Wall Street Journal* describes as "arguably the highest-profile assignment in Chicago's latest boom"—the Hyatt Development Corporation's Park Tower (see pp. 22-23)—as well as conversions of D. H. Burnham & Company's Insurance Exchange Building at 175 West Jackson Boulevard, from 1912, and the Burnham Brothers' Carbide & Carbon Building at 230 North Michigan Avenue, from 1929.

Dennis Lau & Ng Chun Man, Architects and Engineers (H. K.) Ltd

Based in Hong Kong, the firm of Dennis Lau & Ng Chun Man was originally established as Ng Chun Man & Associates in 1972. The firm was renamed Dennis Lau & Ng Chun Man in 1994. With over 330 employees, the firm provides services in architecture and planning, as well as interior and landscaping design.

Initially, most of Dennis Lau & Ng Chun Man's work was based in Hong Kong, but today the firm has projects in southeast Asian countries

such as Singapore and Taiwan, as well as on the Chinese mainland. In fact, most architectural firms in Hong Kong currently depend on Chinese commissions for up to fifty to sixty percent of their work. There are presently fewer than 30,000 architects in China, although Dennis Lau has acknowledged the possibility of increased competition from Chinese architects in the future. In an interview in *Architectural Record* he stated that: "The competition is coming in bigger numbers... than us" (July 1996). However, Lau qualified his ominous prediction by noting that he and other architects in Hong Kong "still have at least five years to [sharpen] ourselves against the competition."

Loebl Schlossman & Hackl

Based in Chicago, Loebl Schlossman & Hackl has existed in various incarnations since it was first founded by Jerrold Loebl and Norman Schlossman in 1925. These have included Loebl Schlossman & Bennett with Richard Bennett; Loebl Schlossman

Donald Hackl (center)

Bennett & Dart with Edward Dart; Loebl Schlossman Dart & Hackl with Donald Hackl; and Loebl Schlossman & Hackl/Hague Richards with Richard Hague and Harper Richards. Today, Norman Schlossman's son, John, and grandson, Peter, are architects in the firm.

With a staff of approximately one hundred architects and interior designers, Loebl Schlossman & Hackl is the city's fifth largest architectural firm. Yet despite its size and long association with the city, Loebl Schlossman & Hackl is not one of Chicago's best-known firms. Indeed, their low profile prompted one local paper to describe them as "the most important Chicago architectural firm you [have] never heard of" (*The Reader*, August 1995). In part, Loebl Schlossman & Hackl's anonymity reflects the firm's philosophy, embodied in the words of Jerrold Loebl: "The reasons for buildings are people.... There are people who provide the funds and are responsible for building. There are people who use buildings, and there are people who look at buildings." Consequently, the firm's designs, which range in style, respond to the specific needs of each client rather than to a single architectural ideology.

The firm is perhaps most famous for its shopping malls, which include Water Tower Place (1976) and City Place (1990) on North Michigan Avenue in Chicago. However, they also specialize in mixed-use, office, health care, hospitality, and university buildings, which they have designed for clients not only in the United States but also in Asia, Latin America, and the Middle East.

Lohan Associates

Based in Chicago, Lohan Associates was originally the office of Mies van der Rohe, the grandfather of architect Dirk Lohan. After Mies's death in 1969, the office underwent a number of organizational changes and was eventually renamed Lohan Associates in 1986. Lohan, who was born in Germany in 1938, left Munich University to study at the Illinois Institute of Technology in Chicago with his grandfather. Another architect in the firm is James Goettsch, who joined Lohan Associates in 1992. As Executive Vice President for Design, he was design principal on Chicago's 300 East Randolph building (see pp. 26-27). Born in Davenport, Iowa in 1941, Goettsch received his bachelor's degree in architecture from Iowa State University in 1967. He began working at C. F. Murphy Associates in 1970. In 1981, after the firm's name changed to Murphy/Jahn, he was named Executive Vice President and Associate Director of Planning and Design and remained with the firm until 1989.

James Goettsch

As the inheritor of the legacy of Mies van der Rohe, arguably the preeminent modernist architect, few firms have had to confront the challenges of Postmodernism as directly as Lohan Associates. Indeed, Robert Venturi's statement that "Less is a bore" was a direct retort to Mies' modernist dictum that "less is more." Nonetheless, Lohan Associates' response has been less dogmatic than might have been expected. In an interview published in the firm's monograph, Dirk Lohan explained that he has "come to slightly different answers than [Mies] did . . . because things have changed. The concerns, for instance, about contextualism, ecology, and energy efficiency are new. Those were not things he was concerned about or even aware of."

Murphy/Jahn, Inc., Architects

Based in Chicago, Murphy/Jahn was originally established by Charles F. Murphy over fifty years ago. However, the firm's international reputation was not firmly established until Helmut Jahn was

Helmut Jahn

named principal in 1981. Now CEO and president, Jahn began his career at the firm as an assistant to Gene Summers, formerly project director under Mies van der Rohe.

Born in Nürnberg in 1940, Jahn studied first at Technische Hochschule in Munich and then at the Illinois Institute of Technology in Chicago. His architectural education continued under Summers, with whom he worked on the famed McCormick Place convention center (1970) on Chicago's Lake Michigan.

The modernist principles that directed the work of Mies van der Rohe and Gene Summers are apparent in Jahn's use of geometry and the grid. However, the buildings for which he is most famous—the State of Illinois Center in Chicago (1979-85); the United Airlines Terminal One Complex at Chicago-O'Hare International Airport (1983-87); and the Messe Tower in Frankfurt/Main (1991; p. 12)—reject one of the fundamental tenets of Modernism in their embrace of contextual conditions. According to Ross Miller, Jahn's work is, in fact, most successful "when it must fit within an established tradition" (*Architecture + Urbanism*, September 1992).

Murphy/Jahn are perhaps best known for their office towers, which revitalized the Chicago skyline in the 1980s. However, with projects in Africa, Asia, and Europe, Murphy/Jahn is also one of the most successful international firms from the United States. The quality of the firm's projects—which include academic, athletic, commercial, corporate, exhibition, and judicial facilities—have prompted the American Institute of Architects to declare that "Helmut Jahn is one of the ten most influential living American architects."

Nikken Sekkei Ltd.

Based in Osaka, Japan, Nikken Sekkei was originally established as the building design and construction supervision branch of the Sumitomo Head Office at the beginning of the twentieth century. In 1933 the firm was reorganized as Takekosh & Associates. Twenty-three years later, the firm was again reorganized as Nikken Sekkei. With almost 1,700 employees, domestic offices in Nagoya, Osaka, and Tokyo, and foreign offices in China, Korea, Malaysia, and Taiwan, Nikken Sekkei is one of the largest architectural engineering planning firms in the world. In fact, Nikken Sekkei has been involved in over 14,000 projects in forty countries, designing commercial, educational, governmental, industrial, medical, and residential facilities. Nikken Sekkei's affiliated companies include Nikken Housing System, Nikken Soil Research, and Nikken Space Design.

Hideyuki Yokyoa

If Nikken Sekkei's size circumvents a single formal approach, the firm's philosophy—"To create sound and progressive designs that firmly take root in the community and achieve harmony with the environment"—provides a general formal direction. An employee of Nikken Sekkei for over twenty years, Hideyuki Yokyoa is the principal designer of two of the firm's high-profile skyscrapers in China, the Shanghai Information Center (1995-2000; see pp. 62-63) and the Shanghai Pudong International Finance Building (1995-2000), both of which reflect Nikken Sekkei's dramatic, high-tech aesthetic.

NORR Limited

Hazel Wong, formerly an associate at NORR Limited, Toronto, earned her bachelor's degree in architecture from Carleton University in Ottawa, Canada and her master's degree from the Massachusetts Institute of Technology. Following graduation, she joined the John C. Parkin Partnership in Toronto where she participated in the design of buildings such as the National Gallery of Canada and the Bell Corporate Head-

Hazel Wong

quarters in Toronto. Her design for the College of Nurses of Ontario Headquarters received the Canadian Architect Award.

For NORR, Ms. Wong's large-scale projects have included Toronto's Pearson International Airport and Skydome stadium. As the co-designer of the National Bank of Dubai Headquarters, she relocated to the United Arab Emirates to be director of the design department. She has other projects currently under construction in the United Arab Emirates including the Civil Aviation Dubai Headquarters, the Emirates Twin Towers (see pp. 120-121), and the United Arab Shipping Company Headquarters. Ms. Wong has recently left NORR to set up private practice in the UAE and Canada.

Novotny Mähner + Assoziierte

Based in Offenbach, Germany, Novotny Mähner + Assoziierte was founded by Prof. Dipl.-Ing. Fritz Novotny and Dipl.-Ing. Arthur Mähner in 1959. The 150-person architectural, planning, and engineering firm also maintains offices in Berlin, Bielefeld, Bozen, and Dresden. Novotny Mähner + Assoziierte's extensive practice includes the design and construction of educational, health care, hospitality, industrial, and office facilities.

The design team of the Eurotheum in Frankfurt/Main (see pp. 108-109) included Fritz Novotny, Peter Natter, and Nikolaus Bader. Fritz Novotny was born in Leitmeritz/Böhmen in 1929. He was educated at the Staatsbauschulen Tetschen Bodenbach and Darmstadt, where he received his diploma in 1948, as well as at the Technische Hochschule Darmstadt, where he received his diploma in 1954. In addition to his professional practice, Novotny is also an honored professor at the Gesamthochschule Kassel. Peter Natter was born in 1943 in Riesa/Sachsen. Soon

after receiving his diploma from Technische Universität Braunschweig in 1970, Natter began working for Novotny Mähner + Assoziierte where he has been a member of the management since 1990. Nikolaus Bader was born in Hanau/Hessen in 1961. He received his diploma from the Fachhochschule Frankfurt/Main in 1990. Bader began working for Novotny Mähner + Assoziierte immediately upon graduation.

Ong & Ong Architects Pte Ltd

Based in Singapore, Ong & Ong Architects was founded in the early 1970s. With more than eighty employees, the firm is under the direction of Ong Tze Boon, Eric Huay, and Ong Siew May. Ong & Ong is one of the few small firms in Singapore that is able to efficiently and effectively design large-scale projects, such as the enormous, mixed-use Great World City in Singapore.

Chairperson Ong Siew May was educated in Australia at the University of Adelaide. Her son, Ong Tze Boon, who is the firm's executive director, was educated at both the University of California, Berkeley and Rice University, Houston, Texas. Vice Chairman Eric Huay, who joined the firm more than twenty years ago, graduated from the University of Singapore. In a profile of the firm in *World Architecture*, Peter Wislocki described the director's education as "a combination of theoretical and practical concerns" (July/August 1998). However, since Ong & Ong specialize in commercial architecture—including the design of mixed-use, office, residential, and retail buildings—practicality is one of their principal concerns. Likewise, the firm's interest in designing with what Ong Tze Boon describes as a "progressive sensibility" is as important to the directors as pragmatic concerns.

Carlos Ott International

Originally established in Toronto in 1993, Carlos Ott International is now based in Montevideo, Uruguay. However, the small firm maintains an office in Canada as well as others in China and the United Arab Emirates. Born in 1946 in Uruguay, Ott was educated at both the Universidad de Uruguay and the Washington University School of Architecture. He was also a Fulbright Scholar at Hawaii University, Honolulu in 1972. As Ott's interest in architectural education includes teaching, he was a professor at the International Academy of Architecture in Sofia, Bulgaria in 1994.

While he has designed projects in Europe, the Middle East, and North and South America,

Carlos Ott

Ott received his most extensive international recognition when he was selected from over 700 contestants to design the Opera de la Bastille in Paris in 1983. The design of the opera embodies Ott's belief that "the architect must achieve a synthesis of the unimaginable possibilities of new technologies and the experience and legacy of the past." If achieved, Ott asserts, "The symbiosis between these contradictions will result in not only a new aesthetic but also a new ethic inspired by the fragility of our ecological system."

Pei Cobb Freed & Partners Architects LLP

Based in New York City, Pei Cobb Freed & Partners was originally founded in 1955 as I. M. Pei & Associates by I. M. Pei, Henry N. Cobb, and Eason H. Leonard. Pei, Cobb, Leonard, and James Ingo Freed had previously been the in-house architectural team for New York developer William Zeckendorf of Webb and Knapp, where they designed a collection of modernist commercial buildings, including Denver's Mile High Center

Fritz Novotny

Henry N. Cobb

(1952-56), a Miesian, steel-and-glass office tower. The firm's rigorous, modernist aesthetic reflects Pei's graduate education at Harvard under the famous high modernist architect Walter Gropius.

With more than 150 major projects in seventy-five cities around the world, Pei Cobb Freed & Partners is one of the most well known and respected architectural firms in the United States. Although the firm received international recognition for Pei's glass pyramid addition to the Louvre (1983-89), it was already famous at home for buildings like the John F. Kennedy Library in Boston (1964-79) and the East Building of the National Gallery of Art in Washington, D.C. (1968-78). One of the firm's other high-profile commissions was the John Hancock Tower in Boston (1966-76), which was designed by Boston-born Henry N. Cobb. Cobb, the architect of the Tour Hines in Paris (see pp. 94-95), received his bachelor's degree from Harvard in 1947 and his master of architecture degree from the Harvard Graduate School of Design in 1949.

Cesar Pelli & Associates

Based in New Haven, Connecticut, Cesar Pelli established his firm in 1977. In the same year he became dean of the Yale University School of Architecture, where he taught for the following seven years.

Pelli was born in Argentina in 1926. In 1952 he moved to the United States to continue his education at the University of Illinois at Champaign-Urbana. Upon graduating, Pelli worked as an associate architect in the office of Eero Saarinen, where he "was not trained to believe that aesthetic consistency is an essential goal in an architect's work." Instead, Pelli was encouraged to consider the specifics of context, function, material, and technology, leading him to later

assert, "Architecture is the art that should change more according to the circumstances." If Pelli's work cannot be defined by a single style, nonetheless it may be possible to associate his name with a single building type. For he is, as Rowan Moore writes, "the preeminent architect of skyscrapers." Pelli's success in designing skyscrapers is no doubt facilitated by his talented manipulation of the glass facade. His best-known tall buildings stand in the two cities that rival one another as the home of the skyscraper: the World Financial Center in New York (1981-87) and the PaineWebber tower in Chicago (1990).

Distinguished among its peers, Cesar Pelli & Associates received the American Institute of Architects' 1989 Architectural Firm Award with partners Diana Balmori and F. W. Clarke III. In 1995 the American Institute of Architects again honored the firm, presenting Cesar Pelli with their highest honor, the Gold Medal.

Perkins & Will

Based in Chicago, Perkins & Will was founded by Lawrence B. Perkins and Philip Will, Jr. in 1935. With the addition of E. Todd Wheeler one year later, the firm was named Perkins, Wheeler & Will until 1944. The firm's first commissions were largely residential projects. Many were obtained through contacts Perkins had as the son of prominent Chicago architect Dwight Perkins.

In 1940 Perkins & Will received national recognition for their work with Eliel and Eero Saarinen on the Crow Island School in Winnetka, Illinois. The firm's success in the design of school buildings led to an astonishing number of commissions. Today, the firm is equally well known for its expertise in designing commercial and health care facilities. Ralph E. Johnson, who is the principal and design director responsible for the

AMA Tower in the Philippines and the Nara Towers in Lebanon (see pp. 116-117), is one of the forces contributing to Perkins & Will's continuing importance as a national and international firm. Born in 1948 and educated at the University of Illinois, where he received his bachelor's degree in architecture, and Harvard University, where he received his master's degree in architecture, Johnson has been with Perkins & Will since 1976.

Renzo Piano Building Workshop

Born in Genoa in 1937, Renzo Piano received his diploma in architecture from the Polytechnic University in Milan in 1964. Following two collaborations, one with Richard Rogers and another with Peter Rice, Piano established the Genoa-based Renzo Piano Building Workshop in 1984. The importance of collaboration continues today in the workshop where design is a participatory activity.

Winner of the 1998 Pritzker Prize, Piano first received international attention for his design of the Centre Pompidou in Paris (1971-78), which he conceived together with Richard Rogers. With a metal frame painted in primary colors and external elevators, the cultural center provoked controversy over its "high-tech" appearance. However, Piano argues, "The Centre Pompidou is a 'celibate machine,' in which the flaunting of brightly colored metal and transparent tubing serves an urban, symbolic, and expressive function, not a technical one."

While important, the Centre Pompidou is only one building in the career of an architect whose work Kenneth Frampton cites as exceptional because of its "remarkable scope, with buildings extending across a wide typological spectrum, constituting a great variety in terms of form, material, and structure." Some of the most

Cesar Pelli

Ralph E. Johnson

Renzo Piano. Photo © Stefano Goldberg

famous include the Menil Collection museum (1982-86) in Houston, Texas; the Kansai International Airport (1988-94) in Osaka, Japan, and the Potsdamer Platz Reconstruction (1992-present) in Berlin.

Plan Architect Co., Ltd.

Based in Bangkok, Thailand, Plan Architect Co., Ltd. was organized in 1975 by a group of architects committed to "innovative and socially responsible architectural designs." To increase flexibility, the firm later expanded to fourteen company member groups. In 1993 the firm added the Humanist Co., Ltd. and the Plan Associates Co., Ltd.; the Plan Studio was added in 1998.

In the July 1996 issue of *Architectural Record*, the firm was described as being at the "forefront" of environmental design, since three of their housing complexes were designed specifically to address environmental concerns. Plan Architect Co., Ltd. has been especially successful at incorporating energy efficient solutions common in Thai vernacular buildings—such as high roofs and raised floors which improve ventilation—into its newer constructions. The firm's interest in environmental design is part of their overall belief that a "commitment to [design] excellence [can] be combined with a commitment to Thai society."

Atelier Christian de Portzamparc

Born in Casablanca, Morocco in 1944, Christian de Portzamparc studied architecture at the École Supérieur des Beaux Arts in Paris from 1962 to 1969. Portzamparc received his first commission to design the Boutray House in Noirmoutiers,

Christian de Portzamparc

Vendée the same year he graduated from the École. However, it was not until two years later, with his design of the Water Tower in Marne-la-Vallée, that the architect was able to articulate his concept of the new urban landscape. Evocative of the biblical Tower of Babel, the building's dramatic spiraling form demonstrates Portzamparc's strong belief that "the symbolic and the utilitarian are at issue in all architectural forms."

Honored with the medal of the Académie Française d'Architecture in 1992, the Grand Prix National de l'Architecture in 1993, and the Pritzker Prize in 1994, Portzamparc has responded to the specificity of urban environments in ways that have garnered him both national and international acclaim. Portzamparc's philosophy of design is embodied in his description of contemporary society as Age III—which follows Age I, the era of the modern European city and Age II, the era of single monuments—an era when the architect "must tackle heterogeneous situations where we are dependent on random forms and the inevitable disparity of today's architecture."

Rhode Kellermann Wawrowsky

Based in Düsseldorf, Rhode Kellermann Wawrowsky is one of Germany's largest architectural firms with offices in Berlin, Frankfurt/Main, Leipzig, and Oberhausen. Established in 1971 by Helmut Rhode, Friedel Kellermann, and Hans-Günter Wawrowsky, the firm now includes Jürgen Weimer, Wojtek Grabianowski, Dieter Schmoll, and Johannes Ringel as partners. Friedel Kellermann is the design principal of the ARAG 2000 Tower (see p. 100). Born in the Rheinland in 1935, Kellermann studied at the Polytechnikum Friedberg in Hessen from 1954 to 1957. He worked for several different firms in Germany until he collaborated with Rhode and Wawrowsky.

In over twenty-five years of practice, Rhode Kellermann Wawrowsky has produced a body of work grounded in what founding partner Hans-Günter Wawrowsky describes as the "functional formal language" of Modernism. Recent examples of their work include the rehabilitation of the Kosmos UFA-Palast Film Theater in Berlin (1998), in collaboration with Konrad Beckmann; the UFA-Palast Theaters in Stuttgart and Hamburg (1997); and Hansa House and Leipzig Park, both in Leipzig (1997). For Rhode Kellermann Wawrowsky, function is expressed by "technical and constructional innovation . . . and new spatial concepts," which produce a "sense of permanence and lasting values." The firm's commitment to a historically sensitive modernism reflects the challenges that architects confront in a unified Germany replete with a treasure of historic buildings in what were formerly East German cities. Rhode Kellermann Wawrowsky's design approach illustrates that advances in technology and construction do not necessarily result in the rejection of context.

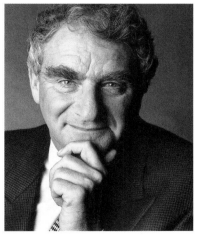

Friedel Kellermann

Plan Architect Co., Ltd.

The Richard Rogers Partnership

Richard Rogers was born in Florence, Italy in 1933. Following his education at the Architectural Association School in London and Yale University School of Architecture in New Haven, Connecticut, Rogers collaborated with his now former wife, Su Rogers, and Norman and Wendy Foster in the firm Team 4 from 1964 to 1966. After Team 4 was dissolved, Rogers practiced with Su Rogers in the Su & Richard Rogers Partnership, and with Renzo Piano in Piano & Rogers—famous for the design of the Centre Pompidou (1971-78) in Paris. In 1977 the Richard Rogers Partnership was established in conjunction with Michael Davies, Marco Goldschmied, and John Young, all of whom had worked with Rogers since the Centre Pompidou project. Central to each of Rogers's partnerships has been a strong commitment to "the relationship between architecture, the environment, culture, and society."

The partnership is perhaps best known for projects such as the Lloyd's of London headquarters (1978-86) and the Reuters Data Centre in London (1987-92), both of which illustrate the mechanized aesthetic associated with the English High-tech School. Challenging the antitechnology positions espoused by advocates such as Prince Charles, Rogers argues that "The problem is not with technology, but with its application . . . when technology is used to secure the fundamentally modern principles of universal human rights . . . the modern age attains its full potential" ("Cities for a Small Planet," 1995 Reith Lectures).

For his contributions to architecture, Rogers received the RIBA Royal Gold Medal in 1985 and the Chevalier de l'Ordre Nationale de la Legion d'Honneur in 1986. His importance to the architectural tradition in his own country was acknowledged when he was knighted by Her Majesty the Queen in 1991.

RTKL Associates Inc.

In 1946 Archibald C. Rogers and Frank Taliaferro established the small practice of Archibald Rogers and Frank Taliaferro, Architects, in Annapolis, Maryland. With the addition of Charles Lamb in 1949 and George Kostritsky in the late 1950s, the firm was re-named RTKL. Rogers and Kostritsky specialized in urban design, Lamb excelled in creative design, and Taliaferro's forte was in client service. Thus, the founders' contributions formed the foundation of the firm's philosophy, which emphasizes design, clients, people, and management. The firm's significant body of work continues to grow with contributions from architects such as Vice President Raymond E. Peloquin, who designed the Warsaw Daewoo Center (see pp. 114-115).

With a staff of more than 600 people, national offices in Baltimore, Chicago, Dallas, Los Angeles, and Washington, D.C., and international offices in London, Hong Kong, Tokyo, and Shanghai, RTKL is one of the largest design firms in the world. Their comprehensive services include architecture, interior design, landscape design, electrical and mechanical engineering, and environmental graphic design. However, RTKL's early success was achieved in city planning, including the redevelopment of the downtown areas of Baltimore and Cincinnati during the heyday of urban renewal in the 1960s. Commissions for single buildings resulted regularly from the firm's involvement in city planning. In particular, the firm is known for its retail architecture, which includes one of the first enclosed retail shopping centers in the United States. However, the firm has expanded its practice to include the design of a substantial number of government and health care facilities.

Architekten Schweger + Partner

In 1964 Heinz Graaf and Peter P. Schweger formed a project team to design the Fachhochschule (technical college) in Hamburg-Bergedorf. The project team, now called Architekten Schweger + Partner, was established as a legal partnership in 1968. Based in Frankfurt/Main, the 130-person firm also maintains offices in Berlin, Hamburg, Hannover, and Karlsruhe. In addition to his professional practice, Schweger is a professor at Hannover University's Institute for Design and Architecture. Schweger's partners are Bernhard Kohl, Professor Wilhelm Meyer, Hartmut H. Reifenstein, and Wolfgang Schneider.

Architekten Schweger + Partner provides building design, project management, and urban planning services and specializes in commercial, educational, exposition, health care, hotel, office, sports, and theater facilities. Some of their latest work includes buildings at the Hannover Trade Fair; others from the mid-1990s are the NDR Television Studios, Hall 14, and the Nord LB Forum.

Peter P. Schweger

Skidmore, Owings & Merrill LLP

In 1936 Louis Skidmore and Nathaniel Owings formally established their architectural practice in Chicago. The firm quickly founded a second office in New York one year later. In 1939 John O. Merrill joined the firm as a limited partner, and ten years later the firm was expanded to include Merrill, William S. Brown, Gordon Bunshaft, Robert W. Cutler, and J. Walter Severinghaus as full partners.

Influenced by the modernist designs of Walter Gropius and Mies van der Rohe, Skidmore, Owings & Merrill achieved international recognition with dramatic steel-and-glass buildings such as the Lever Brothers Company office building in New York (1951-52) and the Sears Tower

Richard Rogers

Raymond E. Peloquin

Adrian D. Smith

(1968-74) and John Hancock Center (1969), both in Chicago. In the 1960s, the firm benefited enormously from the talents of architects and engineers such as Fazlur R. Kahn, Walter A. Netsch, Myron Goldsmith, and Bruce J. Graham. In the 1970s, the firm's success prompted the establishment of offices in Boston, Denver, Houston, Los Angeles, Portland, San Francisco, and Washington, D.C. By the late 1980s, Skidmore, Owings & Merrill employed 1,200 employees in its seven offices.

By the 1990s, many of the firm's high-profile partners had retired. Two of the architects who have risen through the firm to fill the void are Adrian D. Smith, the designer of the Jin Mao Tower in Shanghai (see pp. 70-71), and Roger F. Duffy, Jr., the designer of the 350 Madison Avenue building in New York (see pp. 42-43). Born in Chicago in 1944, Adrian D. Smith received his bachelor's degree in architecture from the University of Illinois at Chicago in 1968. A partner in charge of design in the Chicago office, Smith began his tenure at Skidmore, Owings & Merrill after graduating. Smith's work reflects a strong interest in contextualizing buildings with their surrounding environment through the use of vernacular and classical forms. Born in 1956 in Pittsburgh, Pennsylvania, Roger F. Duffy, Jr. received his degree in architecture from Carnegie-Mellon University in 1979. A design partner in the New York office, Duffy also began his tenure at Skidmore, Owings & Merrill following his graduation.

Sydness Architects, P. C.

Based in New York City, K. Jeffries Sydness established his eponymous firm in 1996. Following his undergraduate studies at Principia College, Sydness received his master's degree in architecture from the University of Minnesota. He then

completed his graduate work at Harvard's Graduate School of Design. In 1979 Sydness joined Johnson/Burgee Architects, the architectural practice founded by Philip Johnson and John Burgee. He was design partner on several projects, including the MacArthur Center in Brisbane, Takshimaya, a retail office building in New York, and the Conrad International Hotel in Singapore. In 1988 Sydness became a partner in John Burgee Architects, the successor to Johnson/Burgee Architects.

Sydness Architects' projects include commercial, hotel, residential, and retail facilities as well as interior architecture and master-planned communities. Rather than imposing a signature style on each of its buildings, the firm is dedicated to providing designs that balance a consideration for context with the client's requirements and expectations.

K. Jeffries Sydness

Jean-Paul Viguier/s. a. d'architecture

Jean-Paul Viguier was born in Azas, France, in 1946. He received his architectural diploma from the École Nationale Supérieure des Beaux Arts in 1970. In 1971 Viguier received the Arthur Sachs Fellowship to Harvard University, where he completed his master's degree in city planning and urban design. While attending Harvard, he won the competition for the redevelopment of the Montauban town center and returned to France.

In 1986 Viguier was awarded first prize by Jacques Chirac in the competition for the construction of the André Citröen Park, the largest park to be built in Paris since the Second Empire. He was also selected by Jacques Chirac as the head architect for the Dupleix district redevelopment. In addition to his private practice, Viguier was appointed assistant professor at the École Nationale Supérieur des Beaux Arts in 1974.

Jean-Paul Viguier

He has also contributed a number of articles on urban architecture to the magazine *Urbanisme* as well as edited a collection of architectural books on Eileen Gray, Gabriel Guévrékian, and Jean Ginsberg. In recent years he has designed buildings such as the IBM regional headquarters in Toulouse, France (1992) and the French Pavilion at the 1992 World's Fair in Seville, Spain.

The Webb Zerafa Menkes Housden Partnership

Founded in 1961, the Webb Zerafa Menkes Housden Partnership has offices in Toronto and Shanghai. The Toronto office employs approximately one hundred employees, including over thirty-five graduate and registered architects. One of the firm's distinguished architects is Brian Brooks, a design partner on the China Insurance Building (see pp. 66-67). Educated at the Kingston School of Architecture in England in 1956, Brooks was awarded the South Eastern Society of Architects' Student Design Prize in 1954 and 1956. After graduating, Brooks joined the Toronto firm of Peter Dickenson Associates, after which he joined the team that later evolved into the Webb Zerafa Menkes Housden Partnership. He became

Brian Brooks (far right) with associates

an associate partner in 1964, a partner in 1973, a senior partner in 1985, and partner emeritus in 1997.

The firm has designed a variety of commercial, educational, and institutional buildings, and is especially well known in Toronto for its large-scale urban projects such as College Park, Hazelton Lanes, and the Royal Bank Scotia Plaza.

Wong Tung & Partners

Based in Hong Kong, Wong Tung & Partners also has offices in Atlanta, Dallas, Guam, and Manila. The original firm was established in 1963, and an international extension named Wong & Tung

Edward S. T. Ho

International Limited was organized in 1975. Wong Tung & Partners also has affiliated practices in Australia, Canada, China, Singapore, and Thailand. With projects throughout the Middle East, Southeast Asia, and the United States, the firm provides a broad base of architectural and planning services.

Wong Tung & Partners has approximately 350 employees in its offices. The firm's managing director, who was responsible for Olympia Plaza (pp. 54-55), is Edward S. T. Ho. Ho was president of the Hong Kong Institute of Architects in 1983 and 1984. In addition to his professional affiliations, which include honorary memberships in the Hong Kong Institute of Housing, the Hong Kong Institute of Landscape Architects, and the Hong Kong Institute of Planners, Ho is also an honorary professor in the Department of Architecture at the University of Hong Kong.

Zeidler Roberts Partnership

Based in Toronto, Zeidler Roberts Partnership developed from a practice that was established in 1880. The firm also maintains offices in Berlin, London, and West Palm Beach, Florida. Its staff of approximately 120 people includes three senior partners, thirteen general and associate partners, four directors and nineteen associates. The project team responsible for the Torre Mayor skyscraper in Mexico City (see pp. 44-45) includes Dalibor

Left to right: Dalibor Vokac, Eberhard Zeidler, Rob Eley, and Ian Grinnel

Vokac, project design architect; Eberhard Zeidler, senior design partner; Rob Eley, project design architect; and Ian Grinnel, senior partner-in-charge.

With buildings in Asia, Canada, the Caribbean, Europe, Mexico, and the United States, Zeidler Roberts Partnership has extensive experience in a wide variety of project types, including cultural, health care, hotel, institutional, office, recreational, residential, and retail. In addition to providing architectural services, the firm also provides interior design, feasibility studies, life cycle costing, master and urban planning, programming, project management, and system development.

Selected Sources

Bennett, David. *Skyscrapers: Form and Function* (New York: Simon & Schuster, 1995).

Cerver, Francisco Asensio. *The Architecture of Skyscrapers* (New York: Arco, 1997).

Condit, Carl W., *The Rise of the Skyscraper* (Chicago: University of Chicago Press, 1952).

Condit, Carl W. and Sarah Bradford Landau. *Rise of the New York Skyscraper 1865–1913* (New York: Yale University Press, 1996).

Douglas, George H. *Skyscrapers: A Social History of the Very Tall Building in America* (Jefferson, NC: McFarland & Company, 1996).

Dupré, Judith. *Skyscrapers* (New York: Black Dog & Leventhal Publishers, 1996).

Goldberger, Paul. *The Skyscraper* (New York: Knopf, 1981).

Huxtable, Ada Louise. *The Tall Building Artistically Reconsidered: The Search for a Skyscraper Style* (New York: Pantheon Books, 1984).

Irace, Fulvio. *Emerging Skylines: The New American Skyscrapers* (New York: Whitney Library of Design, 1990).

Jencks, Charles. *Skyscrapers, Skyprickers, Skycities* (New York: Rizzoli, 1980).

Mierop, Caroline. *Skyscrapers: Higher and Higher* (Paris: Norma Editions, 1995).

Saliga, Pauline A. *The Sky's the Limit: A Century of Chicago Skyscrapers* (New York: Rizzoli, 1990).

Schmidt, Johann. *Wolkenkratzer* (Cologne: Dumont, 1991).

Scuri, Piera. *Late Twentieth Century Skyscrapers* (New York: Van Nostrand Reinhold, 1990).

Viswanath, H. R., J. J. A. Tolloczko, and J. N. Clarke. *Multi-purpose High-rise Towers and Tall Buildings* (London: E & FN Spon, 1997).

Willis, Carol. *Form Follows Finance: Skyscrapers and Skylines in New York and Chicago* (New York: Princeton Architectural Press, 1995).

Yusoff, Norzan. *Tall Buildings of the World* (Bethlehem, PA: Council on Tall Buildings and Urban Habitat, 1986).

Selected Internet Sites

Council on Tall Buildings and Urban Habitat
http://www.lehigh.edu/~inctbuh

The High-rise Page
http://www.xs4all.nl/~hnetten

The Skyscraper Museum
http://www.skyscraper.org

World's Tallest Buildings
http://www.worldstallest.com

Index

Front cover: Kingdom Centre, Riyadh, Saudi Arabia,
    Ellerbe Becket/Omrania Consortium (see pp. 118-119)
Back cover: Top left: Westin New York at Times Square/E Walk,
    New York, New York, USA, Arquitectonia (see pp. 32-33);
    bottom left: Sony Center Berlin, Berlin, Germany,
    Murphy/Jahn, Inc., Architects (see pp. 102-103);
    top right: 350 Madison Avenue, New York, New York,
    USA, Skidmore, Owings & Merrill LLP (see pp. 42-43);
    bottom right: China Insurance Building, Pudong,
    Shanghai, People's Republic of China, The Webb Zerafa
    Menkes Housden Partnership (WZMH) (see pp. 66-67).
Frontispiece: Detail of Jin Mao Tower, Pudong, Shanghai,
    People's Republic of China, Skidmore, Owings & Merrill
    LLP (see pp. 70-71).

Editorial direction by Claudine Weber-Hof
Manuscript edited by Courtenay Smith

© Prestel Verlag, Munich · London · New York, 2000

Library of Congress Catalog Card Number: 99-069134

Prestel Verlag
Mandlstrasse 26, 80802 Munich, Germany
Tel. +49 (89) 38 17 09-0, Fax +49 (89) 38 17 09-35

4 Bloomsbury Place, London WC1A 2QA
Tel. +44 (020) 7323-5004, Fax +44 (020) 7636-8004

175 Fifth Avenue, Suite 402, New York, NY 10010
Tel. +1 (212) 995-2720, Fax +1 (212) 995-2733

Prestel books are available worldwide.
Please contact your nearest bookseller or one of the above
Prestel offices for details concerning your local distributor.

Design and typography by Heinz Ross, Munich

Lithography by Horlacher GmbH, Heilbronn
Printed by Peradruck GmbH, Gräfelfing
Bound by Kunst- und Verlagsbuchbinderei, Baalsdorf

Printed in Germany on acid-free paper

ISBN 3-7913-2343-1

Photo Credits

Our special thanks go to the architects who made illustrative material
available for this volume.

All illustrations are courtesy of the respective architectural firms.
The numbers listed below refer to page numbers.

© Hedrich Blessing frontispiece, 70,
    71 left
Nicolas Borel 96 bottom
Eric Brightfield (Imagefiction) 23
© Andrea Brizzi Photography
    38 bottom, 39
Richard Davies 91
© dbox 42, 43 top, 93 left
Carlos Diniz 44
Etienne Follenfant 96 top, 97
© Jeff Goldberg/Esto 82 bottom, 83
© Stefano Goldberg 138 bottom
    right
John Gollings 48, 49
Andrew Gordon/Fox & Fowle Archi-
    tects, P. C. 37 top
© Gulf News 136 bottom right
© by Udo Hesse, Berlin, Germany
    136 bottom left
Timothy Hursley 30, 31
Holger Knauf, Düsseldorf, Germany
    60, 61, 98, 99, 100 left
Köllmann Aktiengesellschaft,
    Wiesbaden, Germany
    108 bottom, 109
© Ian Lambot 110 left, 111
© Siobhan M. Lowe 134 right
© Photograph by William Lulow,
    Chappaqua, NY, USA 132 right
Misuo Matsuoka 74 top
Nikko Hotels 16 left
Eamonn O'Mahony 77 bottom
Hank Morgan 138 bottom left
Paul Stevenson Oles 94
George Pfoertner Photography,
    Wilmette, IL, USA 135 bottom
Bill Phelps 133 left
© by Markus Pillhofer, Vienna, Austria
    88
Jock Pottle/Esto 43 bottom

Re. PRESENTATION, Incorporated
    back cover top left, 33, 56 left
© Uwe Rau, Berlin 101 top
© Eric Schiller, New York, NY, USA
    95 bottom
© Philippe Simon 141 top right
Laurinda Spear 32 top
James Steinkamp, © Steinkamp/
    Ballogg Chicago, IL, USA 27,
    84 bottom left, 116 bottom, 128
Dan Stevens 140 left
Stuart-Rodgers-LTD. 141 left
© Martin Tessler 18
Uematsu-san 75
© Justin van Soest 72 bottom,
    141 center
Joshua White 37 bottom
Nick Wood/Hayes Davidson 90 left
Dariush Zandi, Total Design, Dubai,
    UAE 15 bottom right
© by Gerald Zugmann, Vienna,
    Austria 89, 131 top right